LSD to Galilee

LSD *to* Galilee

Incarnation in the Psychedelic Subculture

Rob Zahn

FOREWORD BY
Leonard Sweet

CASCADE *Books* • Eugene, Oregon

LSD TO GALILEE
Incarnation in the Psychedelic Subculture

Cascade Books
An Imprint of Wipf and Stock Publishers
199 W. 8th Ave., Suite 3
Eugene, OR 97401

www.wipfandstock.com

PAPERBACK ISBN: 979-8-3852-4680-9
HARDCOVER ISBN: 979-8-3852-4681-6
EBOOK ISBN: 979-8-3852-4682-3

Cataloguing-in-Publication data:

Names: Zahn, Rob, author. | Sweet, Leonard, foreword.

Title: LSD to Galilee : incarnation in the psychedelic subculture / by Rob Zahn ; foreword by Leonard Sweet.

Description: Eugene, OR: Cascade Books, 2026 | Includes bibliographical references.

Identifiers: ISBN 979-8-3852-4680-9 (paperback) | ISBN 979-8-3852-4681-6 (hardcover) | ISBN 979-8-3852-4682-3 (ebook)

Subjects: LCSH: Popular music—Religious aspects. | Jesus People—United States. | Hallucinogenic drugs and religious experience. | Semiotics—Religious aspects—Christianity.

Classification: BV3773 Z38 2026 (paperback) | BV3773 (ebook)

VERSION NUMBER 05/26/26

For my wife, Brenda—

your steady support, your encouragement, your willingness to shoulder the daily load so I could chase this work. You carried more than your share, and I know it.

For Kjirsten, Ainsley, and Felicity—

thank you for your patience and understanding when I slipped into my office instead of slipping a Wii controller into my hand, when I chose chapters over board games, words over hangouts.

I love you. Always.

Red sky at night—sailor's delight.
Red sky in the morning—sailors take warning.
You know how to read the signs of the sky,
But you do not know how to read the signs of the times.

~ Jesus' words found in Matthew 16:2–3

Contents

Foreword

I write this with my third cup of coffee in hand—a humble bean that, according to historian Wolfgang Schivelbusch (*Tastes of Paradise* [1993]), may have helped fuel the Protestant Reformation. Coffee houses became laboratories of reform: spaces where caffeine-sharpened minds argued doctrine, drafted pamphlets, and imagined new futures for faith. Even though coffee wasn't widespread in Europe until a century after the start of the Reformation, this "historically significant drug" pharmacologically supported the rationalism and sobriety promoted by Protestantism, replacing beer and wine in daily life and boosting productivity among the emerging bourgeoisie. History turns on such substances.

Which makes me pause as I encounter Rob Zahn's provocative thesis: that psychedelics, too, have been midwives of awakening. As someone who depends daily on a consciousness-altering substance, I can hardly dismiss the possibility that God might speak through chemistry. The question has never been whether substances can mediate the sacred—every coffee ritual and every Communion cup suggests they can. The deeper question is: which substances, in what contexts, toward what ends?

Zahn's book arrives at a moment when the church aches for renewal. We inhabit a world of post-pandemic isolation, post-Christendom fragmentation, and post-analog imagination, where Marvel's multiverse often feels more compelling than our resurrection hope. Meanwhile, psychedelics are returning to medicine, therapy, and culture, raising questions the church thought it buried decades ago.

The heart of Zahn's project is incarnational: if God so loved the world, then divine presence saturates even the places we have called profane. Scripture itself prepares us for this surprise—God speaking through Balaam's donkey, choosing the foolish to shame the wise, appearing not in temples of power but in mangers and margins. The scandal is not that God showed up in 1960s counterculture; it is that the church was shocked when God did.

Zahn tells this story with passion, and his narrative brims with signs that many of us have been trained not to see. Yes, there are risks and shadows—every revival has them. Psychedelics can wound as well as heal, deceive as well as reveal. But instead of dismissing the whole movement, Zahn invites us to read the signs carefully, prayerfully, semiotically. To recognize the hunger behind the haze, the yearning for transcendence that still throbs beneath the noise of our age.

As a student of cultural semiotics, I see the pattern he traces: institutions often miss the Spirit's stirrings at their margins. The church that once denounced rock music now sings it in worship. The same voices that once condemned hippie spirituality now echo its visions of authentic community and embodied faith. Could it be that psychedelic seekers, like other unexpected prophets, were pointing toward a God already at work?

To engage Zahn's work is to let our theological imagination stretch. If the creed dares to say Christ "descended into hell," then surely no space lies beyond divine reach. The task of the church is not to drag Jesus into the world, but to recognize him already there—in recovery groups, in therapy sessions, in scientific labs exploring consciousness, and yes, even in the psychedelic landscapes of seekers longing for God.

Discernment is crucial. Not every altered state is holy. Not every experiment deserves embrace. But what this book helps us admit is that our neat divisions between sacred and secular may be more human invention than divine decree. That the Spirit moves where it wills, often through means we did not sanction and among people we did not expect.

Coffee changed the world by changing consciousness—sharpening minds, fueling revolutions, shaping Protestant Christianity. If Zahn is right, psychedelics may be catalyzing similar shifts today. The question is not whether God can move through such means, but whether we will have eyes to see, ears to hear, and hearts to discern.

Will we be a church that clutches its coffee cups while ignoring the burning bushes all around us? Or will we, with trembling joy, learn to recognize the Spirit's fire wherever it flares—on mountains, in mushrooms, and maybe even in the margins we most fear?

Leonard Sweet

Author, professor, preacher, publisher, proprietor

Preface

I was conceived in Pakistan.

Why start there? Maybe because that's where this story really begins. Not simply because I was conceived there and happen to be the one writing this book, but because of *why* my mom and dad were there in the first place. They weren't tourists wandering bazaars for trinkets. They were there because that's where the deal went down. Guns. Smuggling compartments. Paraffin-wax-covered hash. A story far bigger than me, and yet the story that made me possible.

From there, the setting shifts to something that feels like the opposite of exotic—my small Midwest hometown. The kind of place that had milk vending machines. Yep, you read that right. When my mom needed milk, she'd send me with a few coins through alleys that cut into Main Street, which looked so deserted it could've passed for the set of an apocalyptic film. Drop in the change, out slid the half gallon. That was childhood.

It was also the kind of town where abandoned houses dotted the neighborhood. The farm crisis of the 1980s left more than fields fallow. As kids, we'd pick the locks on those houses—not to steal, not to smash, but to explore. Dust motes in shafts of sunlight felt like portals, like an invitation to mystery. That's what it meant to grow up there. Stark. Empty. Full of ghosts. And yet strangely alive.

But my most persistent childhood memory wasn't the vending machines or the ghost houses. It was the questions.

"What does your dad do?"

"My dad isn't with us."

"Oh . . . I'm so sorry."

"That's okay. I never knew him."

The dialogue repeated itself everywhere we moved, like a script burned into the social fabric. Over and over. Until the repetition itself began to whisper: *Something's wrong with you.*

What was I missing?

Nothing. My mom provided. She was a teacher. She gave us stability. Dad wasn't there. I didn't know better. It was normal. Still—I had questions. She told me bits and pieces: he was smart, a wrestler, ran a health food restaurant in California called *Millabee Treats*. That's all I knew. Until, in my twenties, about to become a dad myself, I went looking for him.

What I found was an international drug smuggler. A man who lived more lives than most of us could imagine. Who held the initial letter I sent him for *years* before contacting me, only when he was dying of cancer. Who told me stories—or let others tell them—of Afghan prisons, LSD with rock stars, hashish caravans, and paranoia that maybe wasn't paranoia at all.

This book begins there. This book isn't *about* that. But it does *start* there.

Because here's the thing: my frustration with the church runs as deep as my questions about my father. The church has sanitized God, boxed the divine into safe categories, and reinforced the illusion that there's a line between sacred and secular.

That line—is bullshit. BULLSHIT.

The Bible itself doesn't play by those rules. God speaks through diviners and donkeys (Numbers 22). God listens to the protest of a foreign woman and lets her change the mission (Mark 7). God shows up in wildernesses, margins, and outlaw spaces.

My dad's world—psychedelics, smuggling, counterculture, the Brotherhood of Eternal Love—may look like the furthest thing from "church." But what if that's exactly the point? What if God's presence shows up precisely where we're most convinced it can't? What if LSD, music, and surfboards became the unexpected sacraments of a generation longing for transcendence?

This book is not just history. It's not just theology. It's family. It's judgmental questions from people who don't know what the hell they are talking about and milk vending machines in back alleys. It's the ghost houses of my childhood and the ghost stories of a counterculture that wouldn't stay buried. It's my attempt to wrestle with a God who refuses to stay confined to the categories of the clean and the controlled.

If incarnation means anything, it means God keeps showing up. And better yet, it's a God who doesn't "show up" at all but who already *is*—already present in literally everything. In the mess. In the margins. In the places we least expect.

That is where this story begins.

Acknowledgments

First and foremost, to my wife, Brenda, and my daughters, Kjirsten, Ainsley, and Felicity. My sentiments are already lifted up in the dedication of this book, but they bear repeating. This project cost something—time, energy, presence. There were nights I disappeared into my office instead of into your lives. You lost a part of me to these pages, and I know it. Thank you for letting me chase this story, for letting me wander into the weeds of history and theology and family ghosts so I could return—hopefully more whole, hopefully more honest. I love you more than words can carry.

Second, to my editor, Stephanie. Holy shit—you are awesome. For every blown deadline, every ignored detail, and all the chaos that comes with a writer like me—thank you. Thank you for your patience, your relentless talent, the gentleness of your critiques and the sharp honesty of your feedback. You brought steadiness to my mess. This book is better because of you.

For Len Wilson, my doctoral cohort mentor. In many ways, I owe this project to him. When we first met and I came with a few project ideas, he winced. "Good ideas . . . but." Then he said: it needs to be personal—something that will give you energy when the process gets long. So I pitched this story—my dad's story, and his connection to the whole thing. Thanks, Len.

To the friends, colleagues, pastors, professors, and fellow travelers who read parts of this manuscript and told me—sometimes bluntly—if it sucked or not: you know who you are. Your voices mattered.

Lastly, my mom. The reality is this is a story I may be telling—but it's a story she lived. For her, it wasn't a myth or a manuscript. It was real life: the

Hippie Trail, hidden compartments, paraffin-wax-covered hash, even bathtubs full of cash. The details aren't all here (maybe Hollywood someday), but the truth is this: while I'm the one writing it down, she's the one who carried it. She bore the weight of it, and she bore me in the midst of it. For that, and for far more than I can name, I'm grateful.

To all of you: thank you.

Introduction

I am a pastor.

My dad was an international drug smuggler.

He pioneered the Hippie Trail, smuggled hashish out of Pakistan and Afghanistan, and brought it back to Southern California for a profit. He ran a restaurant as a front to launder the money. He dealt to—and partied with—high-profile musicians and actors. He spent time in an Afghan prison. And rumor has it, in self-defense, he may have even killed someone. But that's not the wildest part. He also worked alongside one of the most successful psychedelic trafficking rings the United States has ever seen—the Brotherhood of Eternal Love.

And as wild as *that* story is, this book isn't it.

Because, as I began piecing together my father's story, I started seeing signs—bigger ones. Cultural ones. Theological ones. Psychedelic ones. And those signs pointed me beyond one man's rebellious, drug-fueled journey to a stranger, deeper narrative—the unexpected way psychedelics sparked a spiritual wildfire within a declining American church in the 1960s and 1970s.

Yep. You read that right.

This is a book about how LSD—yes, *that* LSD—lit a fire of faith under the American church. A book about how a generation, disillusioned with religious institutions, found transcendence in acid trips, altar calls, and rock 'n' roll. A book about how the church, even in its decline, was reshaped by a culture it didn't understand and barely acknowledged. Why does that story matter *now?*

Because once again, the church is in trouble.

Once again, people are walking away.[1]

Once again, psychedelics are on the rise.[2]

And once again, no one seems to have any answers. And yet, history hints that these two stories—faith and psychedelics—have crossed paths before. Not just in the haze of the 1960s, but deep in the soil of Western civilization itself—from the visionary rites of the Eleusinian Mysteries, to ancient church walls painted with mushroom-bearing saints, to the provocative possibility that the earliest Christian sacrament carried more than just bread and wine.

Something happened in the 1960s. The use of psychedelics—particularly LSD—crashed into the mainstream, into youth culture, into politics, and, perhaps most provocatively, into the spiritual imagination of America. At the same time, Christianity was in sharp decline. Church membership, attendance, and cultural influence all began their long slide in the sixties. And as religious influence declined, spiritual yearning didn't go away—it just changed venues.

People were looking for something real. Something transcendent. Something that broke through the old and stale religion of postwar suburbia. LSD offered a shortcut—or at least the illusion of one. And for some, it cracked open a sense of the divine.

The irony? The church largely missed it. Or worse—dismissed it. At the very moment people were asking spiritual questions with psychedelic urgency, the church answered with moral panic or cold silence.

But not everyone missed it. In California, Jesus freaks baptized stoned hippies in the Pacific Ocean. In communes and coffeehouses, acid-drenched seekers opened Bibles and heard something new. It was here that Contemporary Christian Music was born from ex-hippies who then swapped LSD for love songs to Jesus. It wasn't the revival anyone expected. But it was real. It was wild. And it was . . . *effective.*

1. Smith, "Decline of Christianity," para. 4.
2. Stone, "Microdosing and Tripping on Mushrooms," para. 1.

Which brings us to this book.

This book is a theosemiotic excavation. That's a fancy way of saying we're going to do what Jesus hopes we do: read the signs of the times.[3] We will read the signs of the past, the symbols of the sixties, the cultural crossovers between psychedelics and sanctuaries. Semiotics, after all, is the study of signs—how meaning is made and communicated. And theosemiotics is the practice of discerning divine meaning in cultural signs. It teaches us to pay attention to everything—from bread and wine to vinyl records and LSD blotter paper.

When I tell people I earned a doctorate in semiotics, church, and culture, I usually get a pause, a raised eyebrow, and the inevitable question: "Semi-what?"

Semiotics isn't just academic. It's theological. It's pastoral. It's prophetic. It's about reading the world, the Word, and the worship of God as layers of meaning waiting to be uncovered. It's about paying attention to the stories beneath the stories, to what's whispered in the background of history. And in the 1960s, the signs weren't whispering. They were shouting.

The church was declining. Psychedelics were rising. The Spirit may have been moving, but we were too busy guarding the pulpit to notice the prophets in tie-dye. Who or what is the church not noticing today?

Let me be clear: this book does not promote psychedelics. Nor does it condemn them. It evaluates them. Historically. Culturally. Theologically. It explores how a chemical compound, when released into the bloodstream of a culture, stirred up new questions about God, consciousness, and community. It reflects on how the church—sometimes despite itself—was caught up in that same stream.

Church

As I stated earlier, I am a pastor. But I'm not a "churchman"—at least not in the traditional sense. I didn't grow up in pews. I don't romanticize the steeples and structures the way some of my colleagues do. I believe in the church because I believe in creation. I believe it matters. I believe that community matters. I believe that retelling ancient as well as

3. Matthew 16:2–3.

contemporary stories about the divine matters. But I've never been in love with the institution.

The church, as I see it, should never exist to serve itself. It should never be the defender of some lost cultural moment or some rigid doctrine of certainty. It should flex. It should listen. It should translate the gospel into the language of the people in front of it—whether they wear suits or sandals, chant ancient creeds or quote Ram Dass. It should know when to move from hymns to rock 'n' roll, when to let the organ rest so drums and guitars (or kazoos for that matter) can carry the melody of the moment.

God

And speaking of God: I'm not here to define God. I hope the word itself is enough to be a placeholder for the mystery it represents. My friend Barry Taylor is known to have said, "God is the word we give to the blanket we throw over the mystery in order to give it shape."[4] That'll do. Whether you're a Christian, agnostic, atheist, or spiritual-but-skeptical, I invite you to read this book not as a statement of certainty, but as a map of questions.

Because that's what this is: a book of questions. Holy questions. Weird questions. Questions like:

- Can psychedelics open a door to the divine?
- Did the 1960s give birth to a kind of revival the church either sanitized or never recognized?
- What can we learn from that era as we face another era of spiritual disorientation?
- And, more dangerously, what if God has been showing up in all the places we were told not to look? (And trust me, I do not even claim to know what it means for "God to show up.")

We'll explore stories—from Good Friday psilocybin (aka: magic mushrooms) experiments in church basements, to baptisms under waterfalls in desert canyons. We'll dive into the lives of people like Lonnie Frisbee, a gay hippie on LSD who became the face of a movement. We'll track how Contemporary Christian Music was born from ex-addicts with guitars and how the line between acid trips and altar calls got weirdly thin. Along the

4. Holmes, *Comedy Sex God*, 149.

way, we'll meet characters like Timothy Leary preaching transcendence through chemistry, Richard Nixon denouncing him as public enemy number one, Aldous Huxley imagining heaven and hell in a single drop of acid, and Johnny Griggs—high priest of the Brotherhood—trying to blend Jesus with LSD-fueled utopia. And we will go further still—back beyond Haight-Ashbury, tracing the scent of the sacred into the ancient world: the Eleusinian Mysteries and their kykeon brew; the curious presence of mushroom imagery on centuries-old church frescos; and the tantalizing possibility that the Christian sacrament itself carries theological, philosophical, and perhaps even molecular echoes of the psychedelic rites of its day.

Maybe—just maybe—the goal isn't to rewrite history, but to provoke a theology and a practice that dares to seek the divine at the fringe, the edge, the margins, and even in the spaces religion once swore were purely secular.

And through it all, we'll read the signs.

That's the task of theosemiotics. To notice. To pay attention. To read the world with Spirit-tuned eyes.

Because sometimes the most important signs are the ones we didn't know we were supposed to see.

Sometimes, Galilee looks like Haight-Ashbury.

Sometimes, resurrection sounds like rock 'n' roll.

Sometimes, the road to Emmaus winds through Woodstock.

Welcome to the journey.

Welcome to the trip.

Welcome to *LSD to Galilee.*

Part 1: LSD to CCM

(Lysergic Acid Diethylamide to
Contemporary Christian Music)

Chapter 1

Buffalo Springfield

There's something happening here . . .
—Buffalo Springfield[1]

Do you feel it?

Seriously . . . do you?[2]

We've all been there—though some of us would rather not admit it. You're alone. The room is quiet. Nothing's moving. But something shifts. You didn't hear anything. But your ears perk up. You didn't see anything. But your eyes scan the room like they're chasing a ghost.

But . . . it's not your senses that are screaming for your attention. It's something deeper. A whisper in your gut. A murmur in your bones. Call it intuition. Spirit. A sixth sense.

Whatever it is, it makes you stop and ask, "What's happening around me that I'm not yet perceiving?"

So I'll ask you again—

Do you feel it?

Do you?

1. Buffalo Springfield, *What's That Sound (for What It's Worth).*

2. If you don't know this song, go to your Spotify or AppleMusic quick and give it a listen. It's worth it and it will help you understand.

In 1966, Stephen Stills did.

Most people think Buffalo Springfield's song "For What It's Worth" was born as a Vietnam War protest song. It became that. But that's not where it started. The spark was a lot closer to home: the Sunset Strip Curfew Riots in Los Angeles.[3] Police had begun cracking down on young people—musicians, artists, seekers, wanderers.

In other words: the counterculture.

They weren't protesting war. They were protesting being erased.

And Stills *felt* it.[4] He saw what most adults missed: that something spiritual was happening beneath the surface. A generational earthquake. A hunger. A rupture. And so he wrote a line that still crackles with prophetic electricity:

> Something is happening here . . .
> I think it's time we stop—
> Children, what's that sound?
> Everybody look what's going down.[5]

But what Stills was doing—whether he knew it or not—was more than songwriting. It was semiotics.[6]

* * *

> The entire universe is perfused with signs, if it is not composed exclusively of signs.
> —Charles Sanders Peirce[7]

* * *

Semiotics is the study of signs—how meaning is made, transmitted, and interpreted. It's not about road signs or billboards (though it can be); it's about everything that points beyond itself to something deeper.[8] A raised

3. Unterberger, *Turn! Turn! Turn!*, 214–20.
4. Doggett, *There's a Riot Going On*, 151–57.
5. Buffalo Springfield, *What's That Sound.*
6. Deely, *Four Ages of Understanding*, 4–5, 72–75, 635–40.
7. Peirce et al., *Collected Papers of Charles Sanders Peirce*, vol. 5, para. 5.448.
8. Barthes, *Elements of Semiology*, 47–50.

fist. A protest chant. A crimson magazine cover. A black square on Instagram. A cross.[9]

Theosemiotics, then, is reading signs theologically—discerning where and how God might be showing up in the symbols, stories, images, and cultural pulses around us.[10] It's where theology and cultural analysis converge.

Jesus was a theosemiotician.

In Matthew 16:1–4, when the Pharisees and Sadducees demand a sign from heaven, Jesus turns the question back on them:

> When it is evening, you say, "It will be fair weather, for the sky is red." And in the morning, "It will be stormy today, for the sky is red and threatening." You know how to interpret the appearance of the sky, but you cannot interpret the signs of the times.

In other words: You know how to read the weather, why can't you read the world?

Jesus was calling them—not to superstition, but to semiotics. To pay attention. To discern. To look beneath the surface. To stop asking for signs and start reading the ones already everywhere.

That's what Stills was doing. He sensed the tension in the culture—the dissonance between official narratives and lived reality—and he translated it into art. His song became a sign. A theosemiotic flare.

And believe it or not, so did *Time* magazine.

* * *

"Time is on our side."
—The Rolling Stones[11]

* * *

Here's the truth: culture doesn't just speak, it shouts. And sometimes, it preaches more effectively than the church.

9. Sweet, *Nudge*, 42.
10. Sweet, *Nudge*, 31–37.
11. Rolling Stones, *Time Is on My Side*.

We pastors spend hours on sermons, meticulously crafting eighteen-minute reflections that we pray will hit home. But you know what often does the job better? A magazine cover in the grocery store aisle.

Enter: *Time* magazine.

For nearly a century, *Time* has functioned as a kind of cultural pulpit—a curated liturgy of what America is thinking, feeling, fearing, or fighting. It's not Scripture, but it is a sign. A mirror. A story-shaper.[12] Covers matter. Each *Time* cover, in its own way, is a cultural snapshot—a collective mirror held up to the American soul. But more than snapshots, they are signs. Semiotic artifacts. Liturgy in print. And if we read them not just as headlines, but as symbols—texts that speak through images, typography, and timing—we begin to uncover a deeper narrative. A theological story, yes—but also a cultural one. A story about what America is wrestling with, waking up to, or trying to redefine. The pages that follow will offer a semiotic reading of three particular *Time* magazine covers. Taken together, they don't just reflect the mood of an era—they trace a shift in meaning, belief, and identity.

Three *Time* covers in particular, from the late 1960s, form a kind of visual gospel for those with eyes to see:[13]

1. "Is God Dead?" April 8, 1966

   A jet-black cover with bold red text. No image. No comfort. Just cultural silence framed as a theological scream. This was not a question for theologians—it was a question for the whole world.

2. "THE HIPPIES: Philosophy of a Subculture"[3] July 7, 1967

   Barefoot youth in psychedelic garb. A movement not of rebellion alone, but of spiritual hunger. A generation looking for God in places the church never dared to go.

3. "The Jesus Revolution" June 21, 1971

   Examines how 1960s counterculture and psychedelic use reshaped perceptions of Jesus—portraying him not as a church-bound figure,

12. McLuhan, *Understanding Media*, 7–11.

13. View the covers yourself at the following URLs: https://time.com/isgoddead/; https://time.com/4835155/1967-hippies; and https://time.com/collections/a-century-of-impact/6291376/jesus-revolution-time-magazine-cover/.

> but as a radical, mystical, love-centered rebel embraced by youth seeking spiritual awakening beyond tradition.[14]

These weren't just covers. They were signs. They were cultural prophecy. When we read them side-by-side, something astonishing becomes clear: in just five years, America swung from existential doubt to spiritual revival. From funeral dirge to altar call. These covers tell a story from the death of a certain concept of God, to the birth of something new. A death. A waiting. A resurrection.

Sound familiar?

And right at the epicenter of that shift—between the decline of institutional religion and the birth of spiritual renewal—stands that jet-black cover.

1966

The year was 1966—just one year before the Summer of Love, and half a decade before *Time* magazine would announce a Jesus Revolution.

Gas was thirty-one cents a gallon.[15] A dozen eggs cost sixty cents.[16] A new house averaged $23,300,[17] and the median household income hovered around $7,400.[18] The S&P 500 closed in February at 94.06,[19] and NASA launched Lunar Orbiters 1 and 2 in preparation for the Apollo missions.[20]

Culturally, the seams were already unraveling. At the Grammy Awards, Frank Sinatra's *A Man and His Music* won Album of the Year, but the Beatles claimed Song of the Year for "Michelle." Paul McCartney also took home

14. There could actually be two more added. The first is a cover from the day after Christmas, December 26, 1969, with the cover reading "Is God Coming Back to Life?" Of course this comes *after* the hippie subculture is identified. Then, much later, in 1977 again after Christmas on December 26, a cover that read "The Evangelicals: New Empire of Faith" was released. It expanded the narrative beyond the scope of this book, but tells an interesting story nonetheless.

15. US Department of Energy, "Fact #741," Supporting Information.

16. Wittstein, "Cost of Goods," para. 42.

17. Csiszar, "What an Average Home Cost," para 10.

18. US Census Bureau, "Income in 1966," para. 1.

19. Buckingham, "Debunking the Myths," para. 3.

20. Williams, "Lunar Orbiter," paras. 2–3.

Best Contemporary Vocal Performance for "Eleanor Rigby"—a haunting elegy about loneliness and forgotten lives.[21] Fitting.

Albums released that year read like a syllabus for cultural change: *Pet Sounds* by the Beach Boys, *Blonde on Blonde* by Dylan, *Revolver* by the Beatles, *Aftermath* by the Rolling Stones, *Fifth Dimension* by the Byrds, *My Generation* by The Who. Simon and Garfunkel released "Sound of Silence" in January and "Parsley, Sage, Rosemary and Thyme" in October. Silence wasn't just a song—it was a signal.

TV also marked the shift. *The Dick Van Dyke Show* ended. *Star Trek, Mission Impossible*, and *Batman* debuted. Walt Disney passed away, and It's a Small World began spinning at Disneyland. Twister hit game shelves. The Super Bowl was born. Ronald Reagan became governor of California. And LSD was made illegal—though that didn't stop its spread through campuses, coffeehouses, and pulpits.

Earlier in the decade, the world had absorbed a lot: the Vietnam War, the Cuban Missile Crisis, the Bay of Pigs, the assassination of JFK. Race riots flared in Birmingham (1963), Harlem (1964), Watts (1965), and Chicago (1966). The foundation was cracking.

And then, on April 8, 1966, came the question that stopped the nation cold. No image. Just three blood-red words on a black background. "Is God Dead?"A cultural funeral notice. An apocalyptic scream.

It was more than a cover. It was a reckoning.

The backlash was instant. Some 3,421 letters poured in. One outraged reader wrote, "Your ugly cover is a blasphemous outrage."[22] CBS aired a television funeral for God.[23] Even Bob Dylan later remarked in *Playboy*, "If you were God, how would you like to see that written about yourself?"[24]

But the shock wasn't just the question. It was the realization that the question made *sense*.

21. Grammy Awards, "1966 Grammy Winners," para. 2.
22. Rothman, "Is God Dead?," para. 1.
23. Elson, "Is God Dead?," para. 6.
24. Scraps from the Loft, "Bob Dylan: *Playboy* Interview (1978)."

Just one month earlier, John Lennon had said the Beatles were "more popular than Jesus."[25] At the time, it seemed arrogant. But it wasn't wrong. It was revelatory. Why? Because he wasn't wrong. He was just early.

Which brings us to the article that dared to ask the question behind the question.

Inside that *Time* issue was an article that didn't just report on theological speculation—it opened a cultural fault line. Titled "Toward a Hidden God," it profiled a handful of radical theologians who were saying out loud what many in the pews were already thinking:

If God is real . . . why does God feel so absent?[26]

This wasn't atheism.

It was honesty.

It was theology doing what theology must do—wrestling with the silence of God in a changing world.

Thomas J. J. Altizer declared that God had died—not in nihilism, but in love. On the cross. God had emptied Godself into the world, and the resurrection wasn't a return to the sky but a diffusion of divine presence into human experience.[27] And Altizer wasn't alone. Lutheran theologian Martin Marty observed that most pews were filled with "practical atheists"—people who said they believed in God but lived as if God didn't exist.[28] A 1965 poll showed that while 97 percent of Americans claimed belief in God, only 27 percent considered themselves religious.[29]

Let that sink in.

The question on the cover wasn't the beginning of change. It was the announcement that something already *had* changed.

25. Sullivan, "'More Popular Than Jesus.'" The full quote (313): "Christianity will go. It will vanish and shrink. I needn't argue about that; I'm right and I will be proven right. We're more popular than Jesus now; I don't know which will go first—rock 'n' roll or Christianity. Jesus was alright, but his disciples were thick and ordinary. It's them twisting it that ruins it for me."

26. Elson, "Is God Dead?," 2.

27. Altizer, *Living the Death of God*, ch. 8.

28. Elson, "Is God Dead?," 2.

29. Elson, "Is God Dead?," 2.

William Hamilton and Paul van Buren took different routes, asking whether Jesus could still matter in a world where traditional language no longer made contact.[30] They weren't trying to destroy Christianity. They were trying to save it—from irrelevance.

But the article didn't just lay out theological arguments. It pointed to a broader cultural shift. Modern people have become indifferent to religion because religion itself has become irrelevant to the real questions of life.[31]

That sentiment should have shattered pulpits. Instead, most of the church shrugged—or panicked.

Because here's the thing. By 1966, the church in America was already in decline. Not in numbers—yet. Rather in connection. In relevance. In soul.

The *Time* cover didn't *cause* the crisis. It *named* it.

Back in 1932, Dietrich Bonhoeffer, a Lutheran pastor who was executed by the Nazis for his participation in a plot to assassinate Adolf Hitler, declared, "The church is dead."[32] Twelve years later, from a Nazi prison cell, he wrote, "We are proceeding towards a time of no religion at all."[33] In January of 1966, just months before *Time*'s infamous cover, *Newsweek* echoed Bonhoeffer, writing: "The future that Bonhoeffer envisioned is taking shape."[34]

It wasn't atheism that was on the rise. It was dislocation. Disenchantment. Deconstruction.

That cover wasn't asking whether God literally stopped existing. It was asking whether the version of God that had undergirded Christendom—patriarchal, institutional, moralistic, Americanized—was dead. And maybe that wasn't a funeral. Maybe it was a resurrection waiting to happen.

One anguished teenager put it this way:

"I love God . . . but I hate the church."[35]

30. Elson, "Is God Dead?," 2, 8.
31. Elson, "Is God Dead?," 1–8.
32. Hordern and Godsey, "Review," 71–72.
33. Bonhoeffer et al., *Letters and Papers from Prison*, 91.
34. Brown, "U.S. Protestantism," 33.
35. Elson, "Is God Dead?," 2.

Rev. Nathan Scott echoed the disconnect: "I look out at the faces of my people, and I'm not sure what meaning these words, gestures and rituals have for them."[36]

The message wasn't that God had vanished. The message was that the church, as it had been constructed, no longer made sense to the people it was supposed to serve.

And so, in true apocalyptic fashion, the veil was pulled back.[37]

What was revealed?

That Christendom was dying. And no one in the sanctuary noticed.

Mainline churches had become temples to middle-class morality. Moralistic, therapeutic, and boring. They didn't preach resurrection. They preached respectability.

And in doing so, they missed the signs. They missed the poets. They missed the prophets. They missed the kids on Sunset Boulevard asking questions the church wasn't equipped to answer.

Time didn't cause the decline of the church.

It documented it.

And the real tragedy? Instead of engaging the questions, the church often attacked the questioners. Altizer and Hamilton were treated like heretics, not canaries in the coal mine. "The 'Death of God' theologians became scapegoats for a generation's religious anxiety. Their theological daring was interpreted not as engagement but as betrayal."[38]

But the truth?

God wasn't dead.

The church's imagination was.

The God-is-Dead theologians were naming something the Spirit had already whispered into the culture: that the old metaphors were breaking.

36. Elson, "Is God Dead?," 3.

37. The English word "apocalypse" comes from the Greek ἀποκάλυψις, which means "to unvaeil" or "reveal."

38. Fiorenza and Livingston, *Modern Christian Thought*, 2:231.

That the divine was slipping the old categories. That something was dying, yes—but something new was trying to be born.

That's what this is about. Reading the signs. Feeling the tremors. Hearing the frequency shift.

When Jesus said, "You know how to interpret the red sky . . . but not the signs of the times," he wasn't rebuking superstition. He was pleading for spiritual awareness.

And in 1966, the signs were everywhere.

In the music.

In the protests.

In the riots.

In the magazine racks.

Even in the empty pews.

Something was happening. Something still is.

The church today finds itself in a moment not unlike 1966. Pew numbers are down. Trust is eroding. Young people are walking away—not because they've lost faith, but because they're searching for one worth keeping. The signs are everywhere: the rise of the "nones," the explosion of deconstruction podcasts, the hunger for authenticity, embodiment, justice, beauty, and belonging.

And once again, the question remains. Remember the question?

Do you feel it?

Because I do.

I feel the tremble. I hear the silence. I see the signs.

And like Stephen Stills of Buffalo Springfield, I want to shout:

> Something is happening here . . .
> I think it's time we stop—
> Children, what's that sound?
> Everybody look what's going down.

1967

* * *

> The line it is drawn, the curse it is cast. The slow one now will later be fast. As the present now will later be past. The order is rapidly fadin', and the first one now will later be last. For the times they are a-changin'.
>
> —Bob Dylan[39]

* * *

The second *Time* magazine cover guiding our journey through the psychedelic subculture dropped on July 7, 1967, in the heat of what we now call the Summer of Love. Its title? "The Hippies: Philosophy of a Subculture." A bold declaration. A snapshot of a cultural uprising. And almost certainly a direct response to the Human Be-In that kicked off the year—January 14, 1967—when more than 20,000 dreamers, dropouts, and seekers flooded Golden Gate Park in San Francisco.

This wasn't just a concert or protest. It was a happening. A communion. A counter-liturgy for a counterculture.

And, of course, as Owsley Stanley gifted "White Lighting"-brand LSD to the faithful at the Human Be-In, *Time* took notice.

This cover marked a seismic shift in America's psyche. Something was breaking loose. Something wild and untamed. And whether or not psychedelics caused it, they were unquestionably its accelerant. LSD stood at the center of the spiritual earthquake. As *Time* put it: "With those drugs had come the psychedelic philosophy, an impassioned belief in the self-revealing, mind-expanding powers of potent weeds and seeds and chemical compounds known to man since prehistory but wholly alien to the rationale of Western society."[40]

The people participating in that philosophy? We called them hippies.

But who exactly were they?

That's a slippery question. The Merriam-Webster dictionary plays it safe: "A usually young person who rejects mores of established society (as by

39. Dylan, "Times They Are A-Changin," on *The Times They Are A-Changin'.*

40. "Youth," para. 4.

dressing unconventionally or favoring communal living) and advocates a nonviolent ethic."[41]

Oxford goes a little deeper: "A member of a countercultural movement which began in the late 1960s, characterized by pacifism, rejection of conventional values, and the taking of hallucinogenic drugs."[42]

It's subtle, sure. But words matter. And that difference matters. Because the hippie wasn't just a fashion choice. This wasn't just about fringe vests and patchouli. It was a spiritual posture. A cultural protest. A generational roar.

Arnold Toynbee called them "a red warning light for the American way of life."[43] And for good reason. These weren't just rebels. They were reformers—though not in the way most Americans understood reform.[44] They rejected war. Embraced sexual freedom. Built communes. They weren't content to critique the machine—they walked away from it. Their ethos? Peace, love, and radical interdependence.

* * *

All You Need Is Love.
—The Beatles[45]

* * *

And central to that ethos was love—not as sentiment, but as a way of being. "The key ethical element in the hippie movement is love," *Time* reported, "indiscriminate and all-embracing, fluid and changeable, directed at friend and foe alike."[46]

Episcopal Bishop James Pike, often dismissed as heretical and always ahead of his time, saw something sacred: "There is something about the temper and quality of these people . . . a gentleness, a quietness, an interest—something good."[47]

41. *Merriam-Webster* (online), "hippie," para. 1.
42. *Oxford English Dictionary* (online), "hippie," para. 1.
43. "Youth," para. 1.
44. Hirsch et al., *Dictionary of Cultural Literacy*, 419.
45. Beatles, *All You Need Is Love.*
46. "Youth," para. 25.
47. "Youth," para. 1.

The hippies were dreamers. But they weren't naive. They believed a better world was possible—one rooted in kindness, community, and grace. A world, as *Time* put it, "rich in spiritual grace that will revive the old virtues of agape and reverence."[48]

But what's truly fascinating isn't just what they believed—it's how they tried to bring it to life.

In most cultures, change comes through power—political campaigns, military coups, policy shifts. Not the hippies. Their revolution came dressed in song. Wrapped in incense. Drenched in color. Their "weapons" were music festivals, be-ins, sit-ins, and acid trips. Their battlegrounds? Haight-Ashbury. Monterey. Woodstock.[49]

Martin Marty of the University of Chicago once observed that the hippies revealed to the world "the exhaustion of a tradition"—a tradition that was (and maybe still is) "production-directed, problem-solving, goal-oriented and compulsive in its way of thinking."[50] And that's exactly it. These weren't politically motivated revolutionaries in the traditional sense. They didn't crave power. They weren't storming capitals or rewriting constitutions. Their revolution was spiritual. Their critique was aimed at the soul of a society that had become mechanized, manic, and hollow. As *Time* put it, "Hippies preach altruism and mysticism, honesty, joy and nonviolence,"[51] and they didn't just talk about a better world—they tried to live it. A new creation. A new ethic. A new way. Their message "washed over America like a tidal wave, erasing the last dregs of the martini-sipping Mad Men era and ushering in a series of liberations and awakenings that irreversibly changed our way of life."[52]

And the soundtrack of that revolution? It's still echoing.

Music wasn't just important—it was central. It was the primary delivery system for the hippie worldview. Their theological medium was vinyl. Their sermons were stadium shows. And their gospel spread fast.

48. "Youth," para. 15.
49. Bustraan, *Jesus People Movement*, 22.
50. "Youth," para. 15.
51. "Youth," para. 2.
52. Weller, "LSD, Ecstasy," para. 1.

> Music was the primary medium for the rapid spread and assimilation of hippie values to the under thirty generation . . . The fact that what had been called an alternative, subversive, and countercultural form of music [that] could, within a few short years, be classed as a genre of American pop music, indicates how music was an effective medium for rapidly diffusing hippie values to the American mainstream.[53]

In just a few years, what began as fringe noise—freaky and subversive—became the dominant sound of a generation. Counterculture became pop culture. And through that music, values like peace, authenticity, communal living, and spiritual exploration seeped into the mainstream consciousness.

Think about it. The Grateful Dead. Jefferson Airplane. The Beatles. The Stones. Hendrix. Joplin. Dylan. The Doors. Joan Baez. Ravi Shankar. The Byrds. The Who. Pink Floyd. The Moody Blues.

This wasn't just a playlist. It was a liturgy.

But as important as music was, it was only a hymnal. It wasn't sacrament. That role was filled by something else in their toolbox.

Psychedelics. Specifically, LSD.

"If grass is the staple, then LSD is its caviar."[54]

If marijuana was the appetizer, LSD was the main course. Or maybe the holy wine.

As one commentator put it, LSD was "a sacrament . . . a mind detergent capable of washing away years of social programming . . . a re-imprinting device, a consciousness-expander, a tool that would push us up the evolutionary ladder."[55] Some even believed it was a gift from God.[56]

Jennifer Ulrich described the hippies as a coming-of-age "youth movement," characterized not just by idealism and peace signs, but by "copious marijuana and psychedelic drug use."[57] And the deeper into the movement you went, the more spiritual the use became. A Southern California study

53. Bustraan, *Jesus People Movement*, 21.

54. "Youth," para. 34.

55. Stevens, *Storming Heaven*, xiv.

56. Stevens, *Storming Heaven*, 17.

57. Ulrich, *Timothy Leary Project*, 17.

found that hippies manifest in three different categories. The third and final category is described as

> "cosmic conscious" hippies who are introspective, mystical and "spaced" (out of communication) and whose drug use is primarily Eucharistic in nature as an attempt to find God. [58]

It is in the hope of finding one's place in the world, maybe the hope of creating a world full of peace and love that the hippie used drugs . . . as a kind of sacrament . . . Anti-intellectual, distrustful of logic, and resentful of the American educational process, the hippie drops out —tentatively at first—in search of another, more satisfying world. Not because hippies didn't care, but because they were tuning into something bigger. Their drug use wasn't recreational. It was eucharistic. It was a means of communion with the divine.

These were spiritual seekers in tie-dye. Not theological scholars, but mystical pilgrims. Dropping out—not to disengage from meaning, but to find it. They distrusted the American education system, recoiled from logic and linear thinking, and went in search of something deeper, richer, more whole. A world where soul mattered more than strategy.

Which brings us full circle—back to the Human Be-In. That catalytic event in January 1967 where tens of thousands showed up not to protest, but to be. To gather. To listen. To turn inward and outward at the same time.

It was here that Timothy Leary famously uttered the phrase that became a mantra for the movement:

"Turn on. Tune in. Drop out."[59]

Turn on—with LSD. At this particular event, that meant millions of doses of "White Lightning," manufactured by the infamous Owsley Stanley.[60]

Tune in—to what really matters. Not profit. Not power. But peace. Compassion. Love. Community. Beauty.

And drop out—not in despair, but in hope. Step away from the noise of a society obsessed with achievement and accumulation, and step into a way of being that centered soul and spirit.

58. "Youth," para. 18.
59. Starbacker, "Tune In, Turn On, Step Up," para. 3.
60. Ferranti, "Trippy Life," para. 2.

That phrase—"Turn on. Tune in. Drop out."—was more than a slogan. It was a theosemiotic invitation. A rereading of the world. A call to pay attention to the signs that the Spirit might be showing up in unexpected places: parks, festivals, basement shows, communes.

But let's be real. For all their gentleness, for all their grace, the hippies freaked people out. To many Americans, they were unsettling. Not because they were violent. But because they didn't play by the rules. They critiqued the whole system—its wars, its morals, its economics—and offered no debatable alternative. They weren't trying to take the reins. They just let go of the horse. Unlike earlier rebels—the Wobblies, the New Left, even the Beat Generation—the hippies didn't want to redirect society. They wanted to transcend it.[61]

And yet, contrary to the perspective of *Time* magazine,[62] they *did* have an urge to reform the world, just not in the way the world expected.

They weren't organizing voting blocs or drafting legislation. They weren't trying to gain office or overthrow the state. They were trying to rewire consciousness. To reboot the soul. To embody a new creation.

And in many ways, they did.

They didn't defeat the American empire, but they did crack its shell. They infused it with questions it wasn't ready to ask—about justice, love, embodiment, truth, and transcendence.

So how did it happen?

Seriously—how?

In a decade saturated with powerful movements—civil rights, environmentalism, feminism, anti-war protests—how did the hippie ethos break through the noise?

One word.

Music.

61. "Youth," para. 23, 44–47.

62. "Youth," para. 44.

Their message rode in on melody. Their values were sung, not shouted. Played, not preached. And that music didn't just entertain. It baptized a generation in imagination, vulnerability, love, and resistance.

And that's the power of theosemiotics. To see beyond the headline. To recognize a barefoot teenager in Golden Gate Park not as a dropout, but as a prophet. To hear a Hendrix solo not just as noise, but as lament. As longing. As hope.

To take seriously the possibility that God might be found not in marble cathedrals—but in incense-filled living rooms, in feedback-drenched guitar solos, in psychedelic landscapes of the soul.

The hippies may not have offered a clean solution. But they did offer a profound question:

What if the sacred isn't somewhere else? What if the sacred is already here—hidden in plain sight?

. . . and that question still echoes.

Do you feel it?

1971

If *Time* magazine's 1966 cover asked the haunting theological question—"Is God Dead?"—and its 1967 follow-up on "The Hippies: Philosophy of a Subculture" captured the psychedelic pulse of a generation in spiritual free fall, then the June 21, 1971, cover marked the unexpected convergence of both: "The Jesus Revolution."[63] Jesus, bathed in tie-dye radiance, took center stage—not in the clouds of eschatological hope, but in the streets, beaches, coffeehouses, and communes of the counterculture.

The print article at the time was titled "The New Rebel Cry: Jesus Is Coming."[64] But when accessed now on *Time*'s digital archive, the headline reads differently: "The Alternative Jesus: Psychedelic Christ." It's a title change, yes—but also a hermeneutic shift. What *Time* originally reported as social anomaly is now reframed as semiotic disruption: the reappearance

63. *Time*, "Jesus Revolution," cover.

64. Mohs, "New Rebel Cry."

of Christ in kaleidoscopic form, emerging not from cathedral ceilings but from California communes.

The cover highlighted one of the most unexpected social and religious developments of the era: the odd marriage of Christianity and psychedelic subculture. Out of this improbable union emerged what came to be known as "street Christians," "psychedelic evangelists," "Jesus Freaks," and eventually, "The Jesus People."[65]

This Jesus Revolution was a "breath of fresh air."[66] It surged forth amid other revolutions—the civil rights movement, feminist awakening, anti-war protests, the pill, and the psychedelic surge. But this movement had its own color and cadence. *Time* wrote: "There is an uncommon morning freshness to this movement, a buoyant atmosphere of hope and love along with usual rebel zeal . . . their love seems more sincere than a slogan, deeper than the fast-fading sentiments of the flower children; what startles the outsider is the extraordinary sense of joy that they are able to communicate."[67]

This wasn't about reviving doctrine, it was about replacing one high for another. To be high on drugs means to have a drug-induced experience. To be high on Jesus means to have a certain kind of religious experience.[68] And experience is what it was all about.

It was, after all, Timothy Leary who insisted that LSD was a legitimate path to authentic religious experience.[69] The Jesus People believed the same, only they'd traded the acid tab for the communion cup.[70] Though many came from evangelical and mainline backgrounds, this movement wasn't grounded in catechism or confessional theology—it was rooted in encounter, the same type of encounter already learned from an acid trip.

David Di Sabatino, a leading historian of the movement, writes,

> [T]he common denominator . . . was a transcendent experience of God that usually began along the hippie quest for truth and ended with Christian conviction. The Jesus People were Christian

65. Enroth et al., *Jesus People*, 9.
66. Eskridge, "God's Forever Family," 1.
67. Mohs, "Alternative Jesus," para. 6.
68. Eskridge, "God's Forever Family," 2.
69. Leary, *Politics of Ecstasy*, 41–45.
70. Eskridge, "God's Forever Family" 2–4, 9.

> experientialists . . . The reckless abandon that had once guided hippies to turn their bodies into laboratories of chemical and sexual experimentation was now channeled into spiritual exploration . . . Where hedonistic pleasures and a heightened societal consciousness were the primary goals of a hippie immersed in the counterculture, the subsequent metamorphosis into a Jesus Freak now offered individuals the opportunity to be co-laborers with God.[71]

As *Time* bluntly stated, "The Jesus Revolution rejects not only the material values of conventional America but the prevailing wisdom of American theology." This version of Christianity insisted on a "transcendental, personal God who comes to earth in the person of Jesus, in the lives of individuals, in miracles."[72]

These were young bohemians, spiritual refugees of the psychedelic age, who once chased enlightenment through acid and Eastern mysticism, but now found meaning in the Gospels and in a personal relationship with Jesus Christ. The Jesus People were hippies who had swapped out the LSD experience for a Jesus experience.

And like the counterculture and psychedelics that birthed them, the Jesus People had no central headquarters. The movement bubbled up unexpectedly, organically, wherever countercultural currents met evangelical outreach. After the Summer of Love in 1967, the movement popped up in Oregon, Seattle, Spokane, Fort Lauderdale, Detroit, Milwaukee, and New York—anywhere the Jesus message intersected with the hippie quest for meaning.[73]

In response to a *Christian Life* article profiling psychedelic Christians in San Francisco, West Coast ministries sprang up to reach youth experimenting with drugs and transcendence. The article, "God's Thing in Hippieville," introduced readers to Ted Wise and others—"by all conventional standards . . . a weird mob" of "psychedelic Christians" marching to Jesus through acid-washed streets.[74] Los Angeles birthed a few of the more iconic expressions: Arthur Blessitt's His Place,[75] Tony and Susan Alamo's

71. Di Sabatino, *Jesus People Movement*, 5.
72. Mohs, "Alternative Jesus," para 7.
73. Eskridge, "God's Forever Family," 55–59.
74. Allan, "God's Thing in Hippieville," 33.
75. Eskridge, "God's Forever Family," 58.

Christian Foundation,[76] Donald Williams's Salt Company nightclub,[77] and David Berg's Teens for Christ—later known as the Children of God.[78] Another convert, Ted Wise, along with Steve Heefner, Jim Doop, and Danny Sands, opened a coffeehouse called The Living Room. It was through this ministry that a young man was found on the street, tripping on LSD, talking about Jesus and flying saucers. His name? Lonnie Frisbee (a story we will pick up on in chapter 3).[79]

While the article in *Time* never names Lonnie Frisbee directly, his ghost lingers in the margins. The story hints at someone like him who exemplifies a new breed of barefoot Christians, as they put it, preaching in jeans and tie-dye, baptizing runaways in the Pacific, and claiming visions of Jesus mid-acid trip.[80] The writers describe these strange young disciples gathering in coffeehouses, witnessing on street corners, living in communes, and proclaiming the return of Christ with the same passion and certainty that others in the Haight had once proclaimed the Age of Aquarius. Their fervor wasn't borrowed; it was raw, native, experiential. In fact, *Time* seemed stunned by their conviction: "What startles the outsider is the extraordinary sense of joy that they are able to communicate."[81]

This joy wasn't incidental, it was instrumental. It was music-infused, chant-soaked, and harmony-driven. Which makes sense. If the hippies used music to reimagine the world, then the Jesus People used music to reimagine God. It was, to quote Hiley Ward, a movement with a "preoccupation with new music."[82] Ward, who documented the Jesus People in Detroit, noted that traditional hymns were rarely sung. Instead, this movement wrote its own music: raw, repetitive, emotional, and electric.

It's in this cultural and sonic landscape that George Harrison released "My Sweet Lord" in 1970, his first single after the Beatles disbanded. By 1971, it had topped the charts worldwide.[83, 84] Though the song was

76. Enroth et al., *Jesus People*, 16.

77. Eskridge, "God's Forever Family," 59–61.

78. Eskridge, "God's Forever Family," 63–68.

79. Frisbee and Sachs, *Great Commission*, 44.

80. Mohs, "Alternative Jesus."

81. Mohs, "Alternative Jesus," para. 6.

82. Ward, *Far-Out Saints*, 25.

83. WorldRadioHistory.com, "Billboard Magazine: 1971."

84. Wikipedia, "1971 in British Music," singles table.

written in praise of the Hindu deity Krishna, it also, as scholars note, "reflects Harrison's often-stated desire for a direct relationship with God, expressed in simple words that all believers could affirm, regardless of their religion."[85] He wasn't a Jesus Freak, per se—but his longing for transcendence mirrored the same hunger fueling the Jesus People. Harrison's stripped-down, chord-light, spiritually thick anthem could have been played in a Jesus People coffeehouse and few would've blinked.[86] His theology may have been different, but his desire? Nearly identical.

The connection here is less doctrinal and more musical—a shared reliance on song as sacrament. If LSD was once the sacrament of the psychedelic seeker, then for the Jesus People, music became the medium of encounter. "To the children of the Spiritual Sixties, nothing was more singularly important than their addiction to music."[87]

These were not songs sung about God so much as sung *to* God. Greg Laurie, who would later become a major evangelical leader, described his first experience at Calvary Chapel this way: "Let's just say that these songs the Jesus People sang did not have a whole lot of complexity. There were about four chords. Simple lyrics, repeated again and again. In spite of the simplicity, or maybe because of it, the songs intrigued me. The kids weren't singing for themselves; it seemed like they were singing to someone. That was strange."[88]

This movement birthed not just a revival, but a soundtrack. What started with local bands like Love Song and Children of the Day soon matured into the early foundations of what we now call Contemporary Christian Music (CCM). Larry Norman, one of its earliest pioneers, asked what became a generational anthem: "Why should the devil have all the good music?" It's a line often attributed to Martin Luther,[89] who himself repurposed secular melodies for sacred purposes.[90] The Jesus People weren't afraid of such innovation. They sanctified the sounds of the street. If Jefferson Airplane

85. Inglis, *Words and Music*, 24.

86. Tillery, *Working Class Mystic*, 119–20.

87. Di Sabatino, *Jesus People Movement*, 135.

88. Laurie and Vaughn, *Jesus Revolution*, 72–73.

89. The School of Wesleyan Studies, "Why Should the Devil Have All the Good Tunes?," para. 2.

90. Luther, *Luther's Works, vol.* 53, 213.

could openly sing about drugs, then a hippie Christian could sing about that which was important to them, namely Jesus Christ.[91]

It's no coincidence that in 1971, the very year of the *Time* article, Chuck Smith founded Maranatha! Music, essentially institutionalizing the Jesus People sound.[92] Over the next few years, praise songs like "Father, I Adore You," "Seek Ye First," and "Humble Thyself in the Sight of the Lord" emerged. These weren't *Billboard* hits. They were sanctuary anthems. And they worked. This wasn't just a revolution against America's moral collapse, it was a revolution against its theology. These weren't systematic theologians. They were sign-readers, seekers, psalmists. They were semioticians. And their music bypassed the brain and went straight for the spirit.

Out of this ethos emerged two parallel music legacies: CCM and Praise Music. CCM, performance-based and industry-shaped, would eventually chart *Billboard* with artists like Amy Grant and Michael W. Smith. Grant's album *Age to Age* went platinum. *Unguarded* crossed over to secular charts. But the deeper legacy might be the weekly reality of Praise Music in churches around the world. "Cutting straight to the heart of the Sunday morning," one historian noted, "praise music proved to be an even more prolific, and controversial, bequest of the Jesus People than was CCM."[93]

The so-called "worship wars" that have split congregations and stirred liturgical debates for decades now, about hymns versus choruses, bands versus choirs, organs versus guitars, are, in a way, downstream from this 1971 moment. *Time* didn't report it as a musical revolution. But in retrospect, it clearly was.

And all of it traces back, at least in part, to that psychedelic crucible of the late 1960s and early 1970s, where seekers of God and consumers of LSD often occupied the same zip codes. Albert Hofmann, the chemist who first synthesized LSD, later reflected, "I did not choose LSD. LSD found and called me."[94]

Maybe, in some strange cosmic way, it also called the church.

91. Di Sabatino, *Jesus People Movement*, 136.

92. Eskridge, "God's Forever Family," 268.

93. Powell, *Encyclopedia of Contemporary Christian Music*, 342–45.

94. Hoffman, *LSD, My Problem Child*, 40.

Because what the Jesus People discovered, and what *Time* inadvertently documented, was that transcendence has many disguises. It can speak in liturgy or laughter, in acid trips or altar calls. It can wear the collar of a priest or the fringe of a poncho. But when it sounds like joy, smells like patchouli, and sings like revival, you better believe something's going down.

In 1966, *Time* asked if God was dead. In 1967, it tried to make sense of the hippies. By 1971, it was covering baptisms on the beach, barefoot preachers in the street, and the soundtrack of a countercultural Christ.

And in the background, always in the background, Buffalo Springfield's chorus was still echoing:

"There's something happening here . . ."

Only now, what it was wasn't exactly clear, unless you had ears to hear, eyes to see, and a heart tuned to the signs of the times.

And Jesus? He was right in the middle of it all. Not just a symbol reclaimed by the subculture, but a living sign among them.

What started with psychedelics, street music, and a whisper of rebellion became a theosemiotic revival. From acid to altar. From Woodstock to worship. From "Is God Dead?" to the "Jesus Revolution."

Albert Hofmann said LSD found him, *called* him. And maybe, just maybe, in some strange way, LSD *called* the church, too.

Because something was most definitely happening here.

Chapter 2

The Brotherhood of Eternal Love

> "They would drop LSD and surf. They felt that they were in communion with the waves, with the ocean, with the earth. So, they called it 'Christ in the curl.'"
>
> —*Carol Randall, original member of the Brotherhood*[1]

Laguna Canyon, 1965–1967

Laguna Canyon, in the mid-1960s, wasn't just a dot on a California map. It was ground zero for something history still struggles to fully comprehend. It was a convergence of outlaw mischief, spiritual awakening, and psychedelic evangelism that redefined a generation's understanding of God, consciousness, and the very structure of belief.

They didn't mean to start a religion. Not at first. They weren't scholars or mystics or monks. They were kids. And at the center of this strange constellation stood John "Johnny" Griggs, an intense, blue-eyed, street-wise hustler from Anaheim, California,[2] remembered as an "occasionally mean spirited badass prone to picking fights."[3] But rarely did he have to finish what he started. Friends recall that although Johnny might provoke

1. Kirkley, dir., *Orange Sunshine.*
2. Tendler and May, *Brotherhood*, 63.
3. Schou, *Orange Sunshine*, 11.

a confrontation, the moment it escalated, "Griggs's buddies would suddenly appear out of nowhere, jump in, and start kicking the shit out of the offended party."[4] Future Brotherhood member Ed Padilla said it plainly, "He was a sneaky, manipulative little bastard. He would usually pick a fight with someone bigger, and when the fight started, everyone would start coming out of the woodwork."[5]

He earned the nickname "Farmer John" during a brief, ascetic period living in the rugged California hills, an outlaw mystic's solitude that foreshadowed a deeper calling.[6] He wasn't reading desert fathers or Zen koans yet, but the terrain was preparing him. He was being carved out. Hollowed. Readied.

In 1965, Griggs heard about a drug that was rumored to be stronger than heroin and stranger than anything on the street: LSD. According to whispers passed through dive bars and biker hangouts, a flamboyant Hollywood film producer kept a large jar of it perched atop his refrigerator in the hills above Beverly Hills.[7] Griggs wanted it, not to sell, not to stash, but to try. To see.

He asked Ed Padilla for a gun. Padilla declined. "No gun," he told him. "Just walk in and slap somebody and tell them you want the acid and they'll give it to you, guaranteed."[8] But Johnny needed more assurance. He found it in another from his circle, who supplied the weapons. That night, Griggs and his crew donned ski masks and gangster coats, and armed themselves with shotguns and handguns. They drove to the mansion, crashed a dinner party, and stormed in. But they didn't want money, jewelry, or anything typical. Just the LSD. The host, sensing the oddly specific demand, handed over the stash without a fight. As the masked men peeled out on motorcycles, he chased after them yelling, "Have a great trip, boys. Jesus, I thought it was something serious!"[9]

One week later, under a star-drenched sky in Joshua Tree National Park, Griggs and his gang took that LSD, an unbelievably massive dose,even

4. Schou, *Orange Sunshine*, 13.
5. Schou, *Orange Sunshine*, 15.
6. Tendler and May, *Brotherhood*, 63.
7. Schou, *Orange Sunshine*, 21.
8. Schou, *Orange Sunshine*, 21.
9. Tendler and May, *Brotherhood*, 63.

for those days,[10] of 1,000µ.[11] They sat on a hill overlooking Palm Springs. And as the drug took hold, something broke open. The experience transformed them profoundly. As the psychedelic effects overtook them, the gang suddenly erupted in a spiritual frenzy, tossing away their weapons, shouting and running wildly through the moonlit desert, utterly convinced they'd witnessed their own burning bush. "This is it!" they shouted into the midnight desert.[12] Whatever John's religious and spiritual roots may have been, they kicked into overdrive. He came back into this plane of objectivity with a single conviction: "It's God! It's all God!" . . . The bedrock realization never left him.[13]

* * *

"I was an atheist until I took LSD."
—Travis Ashbrook, original member
of the Brotherhood[14]

* * *

At sunrise, Griggs did the unthinkable. He returned the acid and apologized to the producer. Something holy had taken root. Something that rewired his understanding of self, world, and divinity.[15] He wasn't just high. He had been cracked open. Initiated. Transfigured. He felt divinity run directly through him.[16] He had seen God.

Weekly experimentation with LSD became a sacred rhythm.[17] These weren't parties, they were rituals. LSD wasn't recreation, it was revelation. And Griggs, once a punk in a gang, had become something else. He was a prophet, a spiritual lightning rod, a sacred outlaw.[18]

10. Bevan, *Brotherhood Hashish*, 35. The Brotherhood's "normal" dose was 333µ.

11. Hirschfeld et al., "Dose-Response Relationships," para. 4. According to this article, a dose is about 100µ. In the study, the dose given that is considered a high dose ranged from 400µ to 600µ.

12. Lee and Shlain, *Acid Dreams*, 237.

13. Schou, *Orange Sunshine*, 24.

14. Kirkley, dir., *Orange Sunshine*.

15. Tendler and May, *Brotherhood*, 22.

16. Kirkley, dir., *Orange Sunshine*.

17. Kirkley, dir., *Orange Sunshine*.

18. Lee and Shlain, *Acid Dreams*, 237.

Church

* * *

"He had seen God while high on LSD."
—Steve Hodgson, member of
the Brotherhood[19]

* * *

In the canyon folds of Modjeska Canyon, California, a sanctuary formed, not with pews or pulpits, but with incense smoke, acid tabs, and a longing for God that didn't yet have words. Griggs had moved his inner circle to this quiet stretch of Orange County in early 1966, and the house they called "the Church" became the spiritual engine of the Brotherhood.[20]

Every Wednesday night, a core group gathered in that space to plan weekend rituals.[21] They called them "trips," but what happened was closer to liturgy. The *Tibetan Book of the Dead* was read alongside *The Psychedelic Experience* and Leary's *Psychedelic Prayers.*[22] Candles were lit. Silence was honored. Scripture, both canonical and cosmic, was shared. LSD wasn't a party drug. It was a sacred doorway.

Travis Ashbrook was one of the first to be pulled into this rhythm. After an ego-shattering trip on New Year's Eve, 1965, he said, "Everything in that book happened to me. It scared me so bad I didn't take psychedelics again for six months."[23] But the call wouldn't let go. When he heard what was happening in Modjeska Canyon, he felt something stir. "They were going out into the desert and experiencing God," he recalled. "I didn't know what that meant, but I felt a yearning to find out."[24]

When he finally joined Griggs and a band of seekers in the desert, the experience cracked him wide open. "The spirit overtook us," he said. "When we spoke, it was not our own words, but that of the spirit, the Holy Ghost,

19. Schou, *Orange Sunshine,* 1.
20. Schou, *Orange Sunshine,* 33–34.
21. Tendler and May, *Brotherhood of Eternal Love*, 64.
22. Schou, *Orange Sunshine,* 35–36.
23. Schou, *Orange Sunshine,* 35.
24. Schou, *Orange Sunshine,* 35.

the holy union. And suddenly I knew what everyone was talking about."[25] That moment marked his initiation.

Ashbrook wasn't the only one. Robert Ackerly, just back from the Navy, tripped with Griggs's crew in Tahquitz Canyon and found himself shouting, "This is God!" while flinging handfuls of sand into the air.[26] Rick Bevan, a recovering heroin addict, dropped acid at Gordon Sexton's place and felt as though he was "remembering something from a previous lifetime." He said the energy was so strong "you couldn't stand up."[27]

* * *

"LSD is always a sacrament."
—Timothy Leary[28]

* * *

The Wednesday night gatherings became the sacred center of gravity. Griggs might have resisted being called their leader, but there was no denying it: he was the sun they orbited. Bevan said, "We were experiencing a whole new viewpoint of life that was so beautiful and loving and caring of others and the whole world. We were plugging into that source on a weekly basis."[29]

They called themselves the Disciples. Not in mockery of Christianity, but in shared hunger for awakening. Even the UCLA psychiatrists Drs. Ungerleider and Fisher, who observed their meetings for months, called them by that name in their psychiatric journal article. The doctors were struck by the group's transformation: ex-criminals and addicts who were now meditating, gardening, quoting Buddha and Jesus, and proclaiming love as the new law.[30]

As Padilla put it, "We started meeting on Wednesdays because people needed it."[31] By midweek, many began slipping back into bars or speed. The Church was triage, recalibration, and revival. It was also unpredictable.

25. Schou, *Orange Sunshine*, 35.
26. Schou, *Orange Sunshine*, 36.
27. Schou, *Orange Sunshine*, 36.
28. Lee and Shlain, *Acid Dreams*, 114.
29. Schou, *Orange Sunshine*, 41.
30. Schou, *Orange Sunshine*, 37–38.
31. Schou, *Orange Sunshine*, 38.

Padilla recounted leading a man named Calvin Delaney into the hills above Silverado, only to find himself welcomed at the Ramakrishna Monastery by monks, then dragged back by Calvin speaking in tongues.[32]

Other stories were stranger still. A Zen Buddhist roshi named Sasaki once visited and used a chalkboard to explain that LSD was only the boat to cross the river, not the destination. But when he finished, Calvin Delaney stood up and yelled, "If it wasn't for LSD, I would have taken a baseball bat to your fucking head by now!"[33]

It wasn't always pretty. But it was raw. Real. Transformative.

Even their founding was mystical. One Wednesday, Griggs pointed to Saddleback Mountain[34] and proposed calling their movement the Church of the Sleeping Angel. Padilla nearly threw up. Then Chuck Mundell, eyes closed, softly said, "What about the Brotherhood of Eternal Love?" Silence. Then nods. Then tears. "That is in fact what it is," Padilla said. "I have an eternal love for everyone who was in that room that day."[35]

A church had been born, not built by brick or blueprint, but by breath, by vision, and by sacrament. And on October 26, 1966, just fifteen days after California made LSD illegal, they made it official: the Brotherhood of Eternal Love was incorporated as a nonprofit religious organization. Their spiritual charter blended Eastern mysticism, Christian compassion, and streetwise idealism. They declared their mission was "to bring to the world a greater awareness of God through the teachings of Jesus Christ, Buddha, Ramakrishna, Babaji, Yogananda, Gandhi, and all true prophets and apostles of God."[36] Article 4-D of the incorporation papers put it even more boldly: "We believe in the sacred right of each individual to commune with God in spirit and in truth as it is empirically revealed to him."[37]

This was no institution. This was fire in the bones.

And from Modjeska Canyon, it would spread across the world.

32. Schou, *Orange Sunshine*, 38.

33. Schou, *Orange Sunshine*, 38.

34. At the base of Saddleback Mountain is Saddleback Valley, which is the home of Saddleback Church, founded in 1979. Gladwell, "Cellular Church," para. 1.

35. Schou, *Orange Sunshine*, 49.

36. Tendler and May, *Brotherhood of Eternal Love*, 65.

37. Tendler and May, *Brotherhood of Eternal Love*, 65–66.

* * *

"One Brotherhood member said it wasn't LSD that changed him, it was the Holy Spirit speaking through LSD."[38]

* * *

Spreading the Gospel . . . of LSD

By 1967, the Brotherhood's ambitions had begun to swell, cosmic in scale and pulsing with a radical belief: that LSD could transform American society into a glorious utopia.[39] The mission wasn't modest. It wasn't local. It was global.

Turn on the world.

Not just their friends. Not just the canyon kids and sunburnt surfers of Southern California. Everyone.[40]

But global awakening required more than good vibes and gospel tracts. It required two things: sacrament and sustenance. They needed industrial-scale LSD and a way to bankroll it. Why?

The acid had to be free. For everyone.

But how does a ragtag group of barefoot mystics fund the distribution of free enlightenment?

Simple. Smuggle one drug to finance another.

They would move hashish, tons of it, because Americans were paying top dollar. Then use the proceeds to manufacture and distribute the Brotherhood's true sacrament: LSD. Free of charge. Divine economy. Streetwise communion.[41]

Thus was born the Brotherhood's dual identity: part spiritual commune, part holy smuggling syndicate. As one chronicler put it, "It's no accident that the most spiritually advanced hippie clan was also the most successful

38. Schou, *Orange Sunshine*, 36.
39. Brotherhood of Eternal Love, "Brotherhood of Eternal Love, History."
40. Kirkley, dir., *Orange Sunshine*.
41. Kirkley, dir., *Orange Sunshine*.

smuggling and dealing operation in North America."[42] Even the FBI took notice, slapping them with a nickname that stuck: the "Hippie Mafia"—a label the Brotherhood wore like a cosmic badge of honor.[43]

It all started small. Grassroots, literally. Marijuana was the gateway sacrament. They grew it, moved it, smoked it, stored it in barns tucked along canyon ridgelines. One day, Griggs showed a friend a warehouse with "fifty tons of pot" stacked and ready for distribution. The Tijuana police chief was on the Brotherhood payroll, collecting a tidy monthly bribe to keep their Mexican supply line open and unbothered.[44]

But weed was just the appetizer.

The entrée? Hashish and LSD.

In 1967, the Brotherhood set off to Afghanistan. They were barely in their twenties. No plan. No backup. Just wide eyes and wild faith. But somehow, they became the first to smuggle high-grade Afghan hashish back to California.[45] That one wild trip opened a pipeline. Soon, huge loads of hash flowed from Kabul and Kandahar to the West Coast.[46]

And here's a glimpse of what that trip was like.

Robert Blankenship (my dad) had a health food restaurant on Thalia Street in Laguna Beach, California. He was from Missouri, St. Louis to be exact. But it was the 1960s, and like so many others, he made his way west. That's where the action was. That's where he met my mom, Gail.

They didn't know each other very long. But one thing led to another, and he invited her on a trip to Europe. A "romantic trip," she remembers.

Eventually, she said yes. I mean . . . who wouldn't?

But once my mom landed in Amsterdam, it quickly became clear this wasn't the kind of European vacation she'd imagined. The traveling had only just begun—and it wasn't going to be romantic. It wasn't even going to be safe.

42. Brotherhood of Eternal Love, "Brotherhood of Eternal Love, History."
43. Dahl, "Skip's Story," para. 1.
44. Brotherhood of Eternal Love, "Brotherhood of Eternal Love, History."
45. Bevan, *Brotherhood Hashish*, 37.
46. Lee and Shlain, *Acid Dreams*, 238.

They joined up with a friend of my dad's. We'll call him Jason. There was a van waiting for them—not a rental, not a shuttle, but a beat-up van that clearly belonged to my dad. He had purchased it outright, in Europe. That alone was suspicious. It was the kind of van that screamed *something else is going on here*.

The three of them mapped a route south and east, planning to drive all the way through Greece and into Turkey.

At the Turkish border, things got tense. The guards stopped the van, which was normal, and asked everyone to step out. But then my mom was separated from the others. She was taken into a small border patrol building and told to wait, alone, while Bob and Jason stayed outside with the guards.

Hours passed. Day faded into night. Tension hung thick.

From inside the building, my mom could hear voices rising. Then, clearly, my father's voice: "If we show you the hole, will you let us go?"

She walked outside to find the van completely emptied. Gutted. Every cushion, every panel stripped away. On the underside, a hidden compartment, an actual hole big enough to smuggle . . . well, anything.

My dad showed the guards the smuggling chambers. At that point, they were empty. Nothing to seize. No law against *potential* crime. Just because you can smuggle something doesn't mean you will, right?

The guard gave a nod. "You can go. But if you'd had guns, you'd all be in jail, including the girl."

That's when it hit my mom. This wasn't a road trip. It was something entirely different.

They were allowed through. But just a few miles down the road, my dad and Jason pulled over. They got out, walked around to the back of the van, and removed the spare tire from the rear door.

Inside the tire mount? Another secret compartment the guards hadn't found.

My dad reached in and unwrapped a cloth bundle.

Two handguns.

He handed one to my mom and said, "They'll never search a woman."

And with that, they climbed back into the van and drove east across Iran, into Kandahar, Afghanistan, and eventually to Rawalpindi, Pakistan.

That's where the deal was going down. That's where it *always* went down.

* * *

The smuggling methods? How did they get the hashish back? Equal parts gonzo and genius. Surfboards, musical instruments, hollowed camper vans—nothing was sacred, except maybe the hash inside.[47] In one now-legendary escapade, *The Endless Summer* co-star Mike Hynson used a spoon from a New Delhi hotel restaurant to carve out foam from his surfboards. He filled the hollow spaces with bags of hash oil acquired in Kathmandu, sealed them with tape and resin, disguised himself with a wig and fake mustache, and smuggled the boards home on a forged passport.[48]

At their height, the Brotherhood was shipping hash by the ton. Hash stuffed in VW buses (that's what my dad did). Pot vacuum-sealed in soup cans. They even ran full-blown canning operations that looked like Del Monte had gone to Woodstock.[49]

But hash was just the fuel. Acid was the fire.

Orange Sunshine

The best acid in the world didn't fall from the sky. It was cooked up in a lab by two chemists with divine aspirations: Nick Sand and Tim Scully.[50] This was no street brew. No bathtub synthesis. This was sacrament science. Precision alchemy. And the result—the golden elixir of a movement—was called Orange Sunshine.[51]

Scully had apprenticed under the infamous Augustus Owsley Stanley III, the sonic chemist behind the Grateful Dead's legendary LSD as well as their

47. Schou, *Orange Sunshine,* 89.
48. Schou, *Orange Sunshine,* 78.
49. See Schou, *Orange Sunshine,* 109, and Tendler and May, *Brotherhood,* 120.
50. Black, *LSD Underground,* 28.
51. Feilding-Mellon and Littlefield, dirs., *Sunshine Makers.*

"Wall of Sound."[52] Owsley's legacy wasn't just about chemistry, it was about consciousness. Scully inherited that spiritual seriousness and scientific rigor. He believed LSD could heal humanity. Sand, Scully's protégé, brought an even deeper zeal. After a powerful mescaline trip in 1961, Sand was converted to what he later called "the gospel of psychedelics."[53]

The Brotherhood needed better LSD. Not just more of it, but better. Timothy Leary himself had said it: the street acid was getting sketchy. Unreliable. Weak. The sacred molecule deserved better. So John Griggs did what apostles do—he sought out the source. Through connections with Billy Hitchcock and Leary's orbit, he met Scully and Sand, two underground alchemists working out of a hidden lab near the Denver Zoo.[54] Sand, trained by Scully (who in turn had apprenticed under Owsley), was no hobbyist. He was on a mission.[55]

In July 1968, Sand brought samples of his latest batch, dubbed Blue Levis, to the Brotherhood's ranch. It was potent, clean, and powerful. He asked to set up a lab on site, but Griggs declined. Too many kids. Too much heat. Instead, Sand returned to Northern California with a deal: if he could manufacture the good stuff elsewhere, the Brotherhood would be his exclusive distributors.[56] And manufacture he did.

Orange Sunshine was born.

The pills got their name from the color, dyed with food-grade pigment to a glowing citrus hue. And it wasn't just a branding gimmick, this was next-level LSD.[57] It came in at 250 micrograms a dose, strong enough to punch through the ego like a battering ram. It was "righteous acid," one dealer said.[58] Sacred in tone. Electric in feel. The purity was so revered that some called it a new kind of communion.[59]

52. Dahl, "Tim Scully on the Brotherhood," para. 1.
53. Bradford, "Brotherhood of Eternal Love Timeline," para. 15.
54. Schou, *Orange Sunshine,* 154.
55. Lee and Shlain, *Acid Dreams,* 241–42.
56. Schou, *Orange Sunshine,* 154–55.
57. Tendler and May, *Brotherhood,* 136.
58. Lee and Shlain, *Acid Dreams,* 242.
59. Tendler and May, *Brotherhood,* 65.

The Brotherhood didn't just sell Orange Sunshine. They flooded the world with it. Tens of thousands of doses at a time. Sometimes hundreds of thousands. Michael Randall once showed a visitor a trash bag stuffed with tablets, casually noting it represented only a fraction of their inventory. "We could have made a lot of money selling acid," he said, "but we gave a lot of it away and funded the production through hash smuggling. We believed we were going to turn on the world."[60]

According to Brotherhood archives, Sand would go on to produce nearly 3.6 million tablets of Orange Sunshine in a matter of months.[61] This wasn't just production, it was proliferation. A psychospiritual campaign to rewrite the narrative of human consciousness, one tablet at a time.[62]

And turn it on they did. One day on Laguna Beach, John Gale handed out 100,000 doses himself.[63] He was the public evangelist for the new sacrament, part surf bum, part psychedelic apostle, dressed in black leather or bright orange jumpsuits emblazoned with "Orange Sunshine Express." Gale and Stubby would roam Grateful Dead shows, slipping tabs into open mouths, giving it away like street Eucharist. They were distributing hope for a dime. Less, if you took a lot.[64]

Behind the bliss, there was serious chemistry. Scully wasn't just making LSD; he was refining ALD-52, a cousin compound he believed produced a cleaner, more stable trip. Derived from LSD, ALD-52 was supposedly legal, a loophole in the law.[65] The goal? A compound that offered all the enlightenment with fewer side effects. And the synthesis method was deliberately designed so that the lab never technically handled LSD, only its legal precursor.

Of course, not everyone loved Orange Sunshine. Glenn Lynd found the trip too scattered.[66] Others complained of intensity. Ambulances followed after the ecstasy.[67] But that was part of the risk. It was powerful, and in

60. Schou, *Orange Sunshine,* 170–71.
61. Bradford, "Brotherhood of Eternal Love Timeline," para. 15.
62. Kirkley, dir., *Orange Sunshine.*
63. Tendler and May, *The Brotherhood,* 115.
64. Schou, *Orange Sunshine,* 172.
65. Lee and Shlain, *Acid Dreams,* 278.
66. Schou, *Orange Sunshine,* 171.
67. Schou, *Orange Sunshine,* 172.

the wrong headspace, power can be perilous. Even so, the Brotherhood pressed on, believing the world needed more light. And this light came in orange tablets.

Orange Sunshine was more than a drug. It was a gospel. A movement pressed into pill form. Made by mystics. Distributed by surfers. Smuggled with prayers. And if it left chaos in its wake, it also left something else: a glow.

A whisper.

A hint of the divine.

Now . . . the Brotherhood needed a temple.

Surfing Saints

Right in the heart of Laguna Beach, sunbaked, stoner-soaked, and kissed by a semicircle of sandstone cliffs, the Brotherhood opened Mystic Arts World, a psychedelic emporium and spiritual storefront on the Pacific Coast Highway.[68] No steeple. No stained glass. It was, as one artist recalled, "the mercantile expression of John Griggs's idealism," a place where acid, art, and spirituality blurred into one.[69]

This was no ordinary head shop. This was altar and armory. By day, it sold candles and rolling papers. By night, it housed trip-planning councils and LSD logistics meetings. Upstairs was a meditation room. Sometimes quiet. Sometimes buzzing with printing presses and pill-packing stations. Rumors swirled that the Orange Sunshine pill press lived there, stamping out doses like a sacramental Gutenberg Bible.[70]

The vision began as a revelation. Travis Ashbrook remembered Griggs "just sprang this idea for Mystic Arts World on everyone . . . 'It's going to be a health food store with clothing, beads, metaphysical books, an art gallery, and a big meditation room.'"[71] But others, like John Padilla, say it started earlier, walking near the Church in Modjeska Canyon. "We need to learn

68. Tendler and May, *Brotherhood*, 61–62.

69. Grundy, "Hippie Noir," para. 5.

70. Tendler and May, *Brotherhood*, 62.

71. Schou, *Orange Sunshine*, 59.

how to make things," Padilla told Griggs. "On an island, we can make things and send them back."[72]

Griggs soon found the perfect space, an old machine shop with high ceilings and a dirt floor. He, Padilla, and Jack Harrington began the build, hiring carpenter Vern "Smitty" Smith, who worked in exchange for weed and specialized in rounded corners, inspired by the *Book of Tao*. "In the *Book of Tao*, all corners are rounded," Padilla recalled. "We wanted everything in the shop to be rounded."[73]

Brotherhood business minds got to work. Michael Randall, a college-educated friend of Griggs, became the store's manager. The plan? An emporium of psychedelic culture: incense, health foods, Eastern texts, surfboards, and an art gallery, with Dion Wright's *Taxonomic Mandala* anchoring the meditation room. The meditation room was the soul of the place. It had foam floors, thick carpeting, a soft waterfall, and a scattering of cushions for seekers to sprawl barefoot. "The meditation room was, on occasion, the private chapel of the Brotherhood of Eternal Love . . . At other times it was the front office of . . . drug dealers extraordinary."[74] This was not a center of protest or politics but of spiritual conviction. "There was no violence," Tendler wrote, "just the unswerving confidence of missionaries going about their work."[75] The vibe was devotional, not dogmatic. Surfboards in the front. God-talk in the back.

Surf culture was sacrament. The Brotherhood called it "Christ in the curl."[76] Riding waves was a form of worship: surrender, risk, and full-body immersion into the divine.[77]

Laguna became a psychedelic Jerusalem. One journalist quipped, "The sun and waves brought surfers, [and] John Griggs supplied a lot of LSD."[78] Mystic Arts World attracted saints and smugglers, seekers and surfers.

72. Schou, *Orange Sunshine*, 59.
73. Schou, *Orange Sunshine*, 59–60.
74. Tendler and May, *Brotherhood*, 61–62.
75. Tendler and May, *Brotherhood*, 61–62.
76. Kirkley, dir., *Orange Sunshine*.
77. Ramm, "LSD Cult," para. 9–11.
78. Tendler and May, *Acid Dreams*, 237.

Hippies danced barefoot in the sand, whispering "Thank you, God" in acid-tinged reverie.[79]

The Birthday Party for Jesus

Christmas Day, 1970. Laguna Beach. Main Beach.

The Brotherhood staged their most audacious happening, a three-day celebration of peace, presence, and psychedelic praise. What began as a word-of-mouth invitation exploded into a spectacle: 25,000 to 30,000 free spirits spilling across the canyon and coastline, baptized by incense, Orange Sunshine, and the wild hope that love might actually be enough.[80]

Then, from the heavens, it rained acid.

A small Brotherhood plane buzzed overhead and released 25,000 tabs of Orange Sunshine LSD, some say tucked in greeting cards that read, *"Celebrate the Birth of Christ with Light,"* onto the crowd below. A psychedelic Eucharist. A holy snowfall of chemical sacrament.[81]

It was liturgy through lavender haze. The poster had promised "The Birthday Party for Jesus," and that's exactly what they got: barefoot disciples dancing in the surf, freak-flag processions winding through the sand, and young seekers tripping into epiphany.[82]

Even the local cops, caught between riot control and revelry, couldn't deny the atmosphere. Sunny Taylor-Colby later recalled, "Everybody was calm and awesome and beautiful and kind . . . I had to stretch my mind and dig deep to remember what happened."[83]

But for the city, it was a line in the sand. Laguna Beach cracked down hard: curfews, camping bans, and an ordinance that made it illegal to "loiter in a group of four or more." Bulldozers were brought in to level the canyon. Cops in riot gear dismantled what had briefly felt like holy ground.[84]

79. Brotherhood of Eternal Love, "Brotherhood of Eternal Love, History," para. 10.
80. Luppi, "Woodstock of Laguna Revisited,"para. 2.
81. Luppi, "Woodstock of Laguna Revisited," para. 30.
82. McPhate, "LSD, Free Love," para. 3.
83. Luppi, "Woodstock of Laguna Revisited," para. 5.
84. McPhate, "LSD, Free Love," paras. 6–7.

The dream was over. But it had been real.

For three ungovernable days, the canyon had pulsed with spirit and sunlight and sacrament. It wasn't just a concert. It wasn't just a trip. It was a liturgy of liberation. A mass for the misunderstood.

And for one flashpoint in psychedelic history, the Brotherhood had pulled off something almost biblical.

They had rained sacrament from the sky.

The Fall of the Hippie Mafia

By 1972, the semi-mystical fog that once cloaked the Brotherhood of Eternal Love had begun to thin, revealing not just a community of cosmic surfers and sacramental chemists—but a multimillion-dollar international drug syndicate.[85] What had started as a psychedelic revival, baptized in the desert winds of Joshua Tree and canonized on the Pacific swells of Laguna Beach, now stood in the crosshairs of the federal government. Nixon's declaration of a full-scale "War on Drugs" named narcotics abuse as "public enemy number one," and with that, barefoot acid apostles were officially rebranded as public threats.[86]

To law enforcement and its newly emboldened task forces, the Brotherhood wasn't a church—it was a cartel. An LSD mafia in holy disguise. "Take out the sources, the main dealers," one agent insisted.[87] And so, the feds did what feds do: they started watching. Listening. Mapping. The long-haired saints of Laguna were now a target, and the trap was already being laid.

Ironically, it wasn't a government sting that broke the Brotherhood—it was betrayal. In 1971, a chemist on the fringe named Brennan got pinched. Facing charges, he flipped. Sat down with Laguna narcotics officer Neal Purcell, whom colleagues called the self-appointed avenging angel of Laguna, and started spilling the sacraments.[88] Brennan knew the whole history: the

85. Bradford, "Brotherhood of Eternal Love Timeline," para. 17.
86. Tendler and May, *Brotherhood*, 177.
87. Kirkley, dir., *Orange Sunshine*.
88. Tendler and May, *Brotherhood*, 176.

hash caravans, the Windsor labs, the coded language and secret properties. Suddenly, the rumors had a name, a structure, a paper trail.[89]

Still, the hardest sell wasn't the bust. It was convincing superiors that a bunch of hippies in sandals had built a global drug empire. "Our toughest job was selling everyone . . . that an outfit like the Brotherhood—in bare feet and long hair—could actually exist [as organized crime]," Purcell recalled.[90] But when intel poured in from Oregon (a seized ranch), from government labs (purified LSD by the kilo), and from the streets (Orange Sunshine flooding campuses coast to coast), the picture became impossible to ignore. They weren't just getting high. They were getting organized.

On August 5, 1972, it all came crashing down.[91]

Operation BEL—the Brotherhood of Eternal Love takedown—unleashed coordinated raids across the country. More than 100 members and associates were arrested. Twenty-nine were hit with federal indictments. Property seizures swept up 546 acres of land, multiple LSD and hash oil labs, and millions of dollars in drugs and equipment. Authorities confiscated 3 tons of hashish, more than thirty gallons of hash oil, 1.5 million doses of Orange Sunshine LSD, and over three kilograms of pure crystalline acid—enough for roughly fourteen million more doses. Even the IRS got in on the action, slapping the Brotherhood with $70 million in back taxes. The media feasted. The mythos collapsed. And in one confused Senate report, the Brotherhood was wrongly credited to Timothy Leary himself—a "cult of mystic fanatics turned drug traffickers."[92]

But Leary wasn't there.

He was already gone.

In 1970, with Leary serving a ten-year sentence for a minor marijuana charge (two half-smoked joints in the car after a Brotherhood party), the Brothers made their boldest move yet: they broke him out. With help from the Weather Underground—a radical leftist group—the Brotherhood smuggled Leary over the prison wall and out of the country. They even paid the Black Panthers $25,000 to arrange Leary's passage to Algeria, where he

89. Tendler and May, *Brotherhood,* 176.
90. Tendler and May, *Brotherhood,* 178.
91. Office of the Judiciary, "Hashish Smuggling and Passport Fraud."
92. Office of the Judiciary, "Hashish Smuggling and Passport Fraud."

landed in the company of exiled Panther leader Eldridge Cleaver.[93] From there, Leary's psychedelic odyssey continued through Switzerland and finally to Afghanistan, where in 1973 US agents captured him—ironically as he stepped off a plane once used by Brotherhood smugglers.[94]

The Brotherhood's funding of Leary's escape, via alliances with the Panthers and Weather Underground, was surreal. It was also telling. These weren't just smugglers. They were true believers. Idealists funding revolutions with hash bricks and pill presses.

But after Operation BEL, the dream was over.

Some fled to South America, Asia, Canada. Others were quietly hunted and arrested for nearly the next forty years.[95] Most served light sentences by modern standards, but the spirit was gone. The supply lines collapsed. The communes emptied. The acid renaissance dried up.

John Griggs never saw any of it.

In August 1969, just days after Woodstock, Griggs died from an apparent overdose of synthetic psilocybin—or possibly PCP, depending on the source. He was only twenty-five. The dose was massive. The moment was impulsive, and the loss, catastrophic.[96]

Griggs believed he could handle it. He was a holy man, after all. He'd stood in the fire before. But this time the fire consumed him. When he died, the Brotherhood lost more than a leader. They lost their heart. Their gravity. Their Christ-in-the-curl. One member said it best, John wasn't just the leader, "John was the Brotherhood."[97]

The movement never fully recovered.

To honor him, Michael Randall and others envisioned the ultimate tribute: produce ten kilograms of LSD, 100 million doses, to flood the world with cosmic light in Griggs's name.[98] But Operation BEL swept that vision away before it could materialize.

93. Kirkley, dir., *Orange Sunshine.*
94. Schou, *Orange Sunshine,* 270.
95. Schou, "'Hippie Mafia,'" para. 1.
96. Schou, *Orange Sunshine,* 191.
97. Schou, *Orange Sunshine,* 192.
98. Kirkley, dir., *Orange Sunshine.*

Still, not all was lost.

Griggs's widow, Carol, affectionately called the "Godmother" of the Brotherhood, carried his legacy forward. She had been there from the beginning, a steady presence in the chaos. Unlike some who would eventually trade LSD for the waters of Calvary Chapel baptisms, Carol never drifted into the Jesus Movement. Her path was quieter, steadier—holding space for the memory of Griggs while others went chasing new spiritual awakenings.

Even so, the overlap was impossible to miss. In Orange County, Calvary Chapel was baptizing barefoot hippies by the thousands. LSD dealers became street preachers. Acid evangelists became born-again believers. Pastor Chuck Smith would later reflect on the street scene in Laguna, where "the Brotherhood had their LSD evangelists out trying to turn kids onto acid," even as Smith's team tried to turn them to Jesus.[99]

It was a spiritual arms race.

One young seeker, Oden Fong, son of a Hollywood actor, nearly died on an LSD overdose. Instead, he claimed to see Christ in a blinding vision and turned to Christianity. "Satan was after him," Smith said, "but the Lord won".[100]

Even Timothy Leary, ever the provocateur, quipped later that LSD might stand for "Lord, See Daddy!"—a wink at the religious revival sweeping up his former disciples.

The Brotherhood of Eternal Love, like all great awakenings, burned bright and burned fast. What started as a church, became a movement, became a myth, became a memory. And somewhere in between . . . it got complicated. They had begun with sacred intent—to awaken a generation, to commune with God through chemistry—and now they were being labeled narco-terrorists. The state had no category for sacramental hash or psychedelic liturgy. No theological framework for a church that distributed acid instead of communion wafers. The only language it knew was criminal. And so the Brotherhood was silenced under indictments and headlines.

Yet perhaps the deepest cut came from within.

99. Beeler, "Generation Led," para. 4.

100. Beeler, "Generation Led," para. 4.

When Timothy Leary, the movement's wild-haired Moses, had been sprung from prison by the Brotherhood, he fled first to Algeria, then to Switzerland, and finally to Afghanistan. But when US agents recaptured him in Kabul in 1973, the final betrayal came: Leary flipped. Facing a long sentence, he turned state's witness and gave up names, locations, and Brotherhood ties. For many, it was shattering. It felt like the prophet had broken the tablets himself.[101]

In the rearview mirror, the Brotherhood looks less like a cult and more like a cultural fault line. A gang of petty criminals turned psychedelic prophets. A crew of barefoot evangelists who tried to midwife the Age of Aquarius into being. They saw LSD not just as a chemical, but as a catalyst, an accelerant for human evolution. Law enforcement saw a cartel. The Brothers saw communion.

Even their peers had mixed feelings. Owsley Stanley, the famed Bay Area chemist, called them "a bunch of loose cannons on a ship of fools."[102] Richard Alpert, later Ram Dass, said they "had the tiger by the tail."[103] That's the danger of sacraments with teeth. LSD can expand your consciousness—or consume it.

And yet . . . the dream lingers.

Fifty years later, their wild-eyed hope that psychedelics could heal, awaken, transform, is no longer fringe. Psilocybin trials at Johns Hopkins.[104] End-of-life LSD therapy.[105] Mainstream publications exploring "ego death" and transcendence. The very vision once criminalized is now being tested in clinical labs.

Maybe the Brotherhood was ahead of its time. Or maybe they were simply a product of it.

Books. Documentaries. Films. The story has been told and retold, often poorly, sometimes sensationally. But surviving members like Michael and Carol Randall have stepped forward, hoping to reclaim the narrative. To remind the world that, at its core, the Brotherhood wasn't about cash or

101. Schou, *Orange Sunshine*, 269–72.
102. Schou, *Orange Sunshine*, 61.
103. Schou, *Orange Sunshine*, 144.
104. Johns Hopkins Medicine, "Center for Psychedelic Research," para. 2.
105. Rosenbaum et al., "Psychedelics for Psychological Distress," para. 1.

contraband. It was about conviction, a genuine belief that the veil could be lifted, that the world could be transfigured.

And maybe, just maybe, it was.

The Brotherhood believed that if enough people took enough LSD, they could create a utopian society and demonstrate to the world the healing powers of LSD. In the process, they broke laws. They broke taboos. And yes, they broke some lives. "The price we paid was far more than any of us expected," Rick Bevan later admitted.[106] But they never stopped believing that what they were doing had meaning. That the sacred could shimmer through chemistry. That they were, in the truest sense, holy outlaws.

The Brotherhood's story is caution and wonder. Caution, because idealism can curdle into hubris. Wonder, because for a brief, beautiful window, a group of kids believed they could turn on the world and bring it to the light.

As one former member put it, "The Brotherhood were manufacturing LSD and had their evangelists out in the streets . . . But the Lord was after those kids too."[107]

Maybe both are true.

Maybe they were right to believe.

106. Doherty, "Dead End Kids on Acid," para. 20.

107. Beeler, "Generation Led," para. 4.

Chapter 3

Lonnie & Chuck

"The Jesus People movement's effects are so significant that many scholars believe it should be considered a fourth great awakening."
—Jordan Monson[1]

Jesus People

The Jesus People didn't begin with a bang. There was no denominational blueprint. No strategic launch. No singular founder casting vision from a stage. They emerged quietly, almost invisibly—threaded through communes, coffeehouses, concerts, and street corners.[2] What began as a scattered awakening among burned-out hippies became, in time, a full-blown movement. Not overnight, but unmistakably. One day, there were a few long-haired kids talking about Jesus on the beach.[3] The next, it was baptisms in the ocean and revival in the headlines.

By the early 1970s, the Jesus People had become one of the most unexpected spiritual movements of the century. They were barefoot mystics and tie-dye prophets, baptizing each other in the Pacific and preaching with guitars slung across their backs. The press dubbed them "Jesus Freaks"[4]—

1. Monson, "Jesus People and the Vibe Shift."
2. Eskridge, "God's Forever Family," 2.
3. Mohs, "Alternative Jesus," para. 14.
4. Bustraan, *Jesus People Movement*, 31.

not as an insult, but as a cultural category that didn't exist until then.[5] *Time* magazine's June 1971 cover captured it perfectly: a psychedelic Jesus and the headline "The Jesus Revolution."[6] The article gushed with surprise at the movement's "extraordinary sense of joy," calling their love "more sincere than a slogan."

But what united them wasn't doctrine. It wasn't dogma. It was experience. David Di Sabatino said it best: "The common denominator . . . was a transcendent experience of God that usually began along the hippie quest for truth and ended with Christian conviction."[7] These were spiritual experimentalists who had traded acid for Jesus and called it the better trip.[8] And while theologies varied wildly, what linked them was a belief in a personal God—real, relational, and active. As *Time* noted, this was a movement that rejected "the prevailing wisdom of American theology" and replaced it with "a transcendental, personal God" who moved through miracles and lives, not liturgy, doctrine, or dogma.[9]

The Jesus People sprouted up everywhere—coffeehouses in San Francisco, communes in Oregon, nightclubs in LA, back-alley pulpits in New York. There was no center, no council, no cathedral. Just flickers of Spirit breaking loose across the map.[10]

And yet, there *is* a gravitational pull in the story.[11]

It bends toward a barefoot street preacher named Lonnie Frisbee. And it converges with a conservative pastor named Chuck Smith. When their lives collided in 1968, Calvary Chapel was just a sleepy church of maybe 200. But when Frisbee showed up, he brought the fire. And Smith gave it structure.

5. *Rolling Stone*, "Peter Green to Emulate Christ?," para. 22.

6. Mohs, "Alternative Jesus."

7. Di Sabatino, *Jesus People Movement*, 5.

8. Enroth et al., *Jesus People*, 10.

9. Mohs, "Alternative Jesus," para. 7.

10. Eskridge, "God's Forever Family," 2.

11. The story of the "Jesus People" is complex. There are plenty of resources that dive deep into the topic. Here, however, we will use the true story of Lonnie Frisbee as a metaphor that helps us have a concept for the whole. But Lonnie's story is most certainly not the only story that could be told to give some perspective on who the Jesus People were and how the movement may have started.

Together, they catalyzed what became ground zero for the Jesus Movement and of course the music that came with it.[12]

The movement had many moments and faces. But did it have a flashpoint?

If so, it might just be the day Chuck handed Lonnie the mic.

* * *

> "We had communities of people who believed in LSD as a religion . . . We'd go out to wilderness places and all take LSD."
>
> —Lonnie Frisbee[13]

* * *

Lonnie

Lonnie Frisbee's story doesn't begin in a church. It begins in a wound. Born in 1949, Lonnie entered a world that taught him early that some things break before they're built. His father, Ray—a honky-tonk crooner with too much booze and too little restraint—abused Lonnie's mother and disappeared before the kid could form full sentences.[14] That kind of abandonment doesn't just create distance. It creates an ache. Lonnie carried that ache like a second skin.

And ache makes people search. For love. For truth. For somewhere to land when nothing feels safe. Before he found a Bible or a pulpit or a beachside baptism, Lonnie was brutalized by someone trusted—a teenage babysitter who molested him repeatedly. The trauma didn't stay silent, but the family did. Lonnie spoke up, and nothing changed.[15] So he ran. Toward something. Or maybe away. Either way, he kept moving.

He moved with creativity and a strange spiritual fire. At Corona Del Mar High School in Costa Mesa, Lonnie got involved in the arts—drama, dance, and design. In 1966, he even appeared as a dancer on the Casey

12. Frisbee and Sachs, *Jesus Revolution*, 68.
13. Frisbee and Sachs, *Jesus Revolution*, 33.
14. Frisbee and Sachs, *Jesus Revolution*, 13.
15. Salter, "Lonnie Frisbee," para. 4.

Kasem show *Shebang*.[16] But even then, something deeper was stirring. By age fifteen, he dropped out and drifted north to Haight-Ashbury, where he enrolled briefly at the Academy of Art and threw himself into a different kind of education—psychedelics, Scripture, and the swirling mysticism of a generation in revolt.[17]

By this time, Lonnie was already done waiting for the church to make space for a kid like him. So he found belonging in the only places that welcomed the wounded: the counterculture, acid trips, and the sprawling spiritual buffet of 1960s California. At some point, he traveled south to Laguna Beach, which became a spiritual laboratory of sorts. There, he tripped with seekers, painted apocalyptic murals in seaside caves, and read Revelation like it was a cosmic treasure map. He cracked Scripture open like a portal, hungry not just for answers but for vision. He wasn't trying to get high. He was trying to see.[18] For Lonnie, LSD wasn't a party drug—it was a sacrament. And the Brotherhood of Eternal Love supplied the chemicals.[19]

And then came Tahquitz Canyon.

High on what was likely the Brotherhood's proprietary acid, naked under the desert stars, surrounded by ancient stone, Lonnie did something that sounded more like Ezekiel than Anaheim: he cried out for God to show up.[20] "God, if you're really real reveal yourself to me!"[21] And God did. Not as metaphor. Not as theory. But as Jesus—radiant, unmistakable, personal. In his own words in an interview, he said, "When the Lord called me I was going into the desert and I was taking off all my clothes . . . and the whole atmosphere of this canyon that I was in starts to tingle and get light and it started to change and I'm just goin' . . . 'Uh oh'. I didn't want to be there . . . then the lord showed me that he was placing a light on me and I was going to go bear the Word of the Lord."[22] Jesus showed up for Lonnie on an acid trip and told him to reach out to young people for Jesus.[23]

16. Frisbee and Sachs, *Great Commission*, 13.
17. Eskridge, "God's Forever Family," 66.
18. Frisbee and Sachs, *Great Commission*, 41–42.
19. Frisbee and Sachs, *Great Commission*, 33.
20. Eskridge, "God's Forever Family," 33.
21. Di Sabatino, dir., *Frisbee*.
22. Di Sabatino, dir., *Frisbee*.
23. Frisbee and Sachs, *Great Commission*, 41–43.

That vision wasn't just ecstasy. It was a call. A commissioning. A cosmic assignment.

* * *

> "I took my LSD and laid down on the floor for a couple of hours. When I could get up, I got up as a Christian. It was just that simple."
>
> —Steve Hefner[24]

* * *

Later, someone who tripped with Lonnie remembered another pilgrimage to the canyon like this: "We hiked out to Tahquitz Falls . . . he opened his backpack, spread out LSD, marijuana, oil paints, and painted a full-size Jesus on the rock. Then he pulled out his Bible and said, 'We're going to read now.' He read about John the Baptist—and then he baptized us. At Tahquitz Falls. On acid."[25] It wasn't metaphor. It was embodiment. Jesus on the rock. Kids in the river. Baptized not just in water—but in visions.

Not long after that encounter, Lonnie hitchhiked back up the Haight-Ashbury area and met Ted Wise—a former surfer and LSD user who had recently found Jesus in San Francisco.[26] Wise, one of the earliest "Jesus Freaks," didn't shed the long hair, the sandals, or the street vibe. His authenticity struck Lonnie like lightning. "Ted Wise told me, 'Lonnie, you don't have to clean yourself up for God. Just follow Jesus and let Him do it.'" That conversation gave Lonnie permission to bring all of himself—his wounds, his weirdness, his wonder—into his calling. God was raising up a new kind of witness.[27]

From that moment forward, Lonnie saw the world differently. The Bible wasn't just a book—it was a living script he'd been written into. He began preaching on sidewalks and praying for strangers, giving a home to the spiritually homeless. "We didn't pass out tracts," he said. "We passed out towels to dry people after we baptized them in the ocean."[28]

24. Di Sabatino, dir., *Frisbee.*
25. Di Sabatino, dir., *Frisbee.*
26. Enroth et al., *Jesus People*, 13.
27. Frisbee and Sachs, *Great Commission*, 44.
28. Di Sabatino, dir., *Frisbee.*

He soon became a spiritual magnet. Lonnie moved into the House of Acts in Novato, California—a Christian commune that felt like the book of Acts via Haight-Ashbury. It was loud. Messy. Electric. Every night there were people getting saved, filled with the Holy Spirit, and healed of diseases.[29] Lonnie wasn't trained, licensed, or credentialed. He was just anointed.

During that season, he dated Connie, a fellow seeker with her own need for a feeling of safety. "I couldn't get enough of their love," she said.[30] Ultimately, Lonnie and Connie married and then hitchhiked south, following what Lonnie called divine breadcrumbs. Their path eventually led them to Costa Mesa.[31]

That's where Janette entered the picture.

Janette Smith was the daughter of Chuck Smith—a conservative, Bible-teaching pastor with a small congregation called Calvary Chapel.[32] When Janette met Lonnie and Connie, she was so moved by their joy and intensity that she begged her father to meet them.[33] Chuck hesitated. But Janette insisted, "Dad, you've got to hear him talk about Jesus."[34]

So Chuck agreed.

When he first laid eyes on Lonnie—barefoot, long-haired, radiant with joy—he didn't know what to think.[35] But, ultimately, he gave him a microphone.

That's when everything changed.

* * *

"No more LSD for me. I met a man from Galilee."

—Larry Norman[36]

* * *

29. Eskridge, "God's Forever Family," 38.
30. Eskridge, "God's Forever Family," 38.
31. Eskridge, "God's Forever Family," 70.
32. Salter, "Lonnie Frisbee," para. 10.
33. Frisbee and Sachs, *Great Commission*, 66–67.
34. Di Sabatino, dir., *Frisbee.*
35. Eskridge, "God's Forever Family," 70.
36. Norman, *Street Level.*

Chuck

Chuck Smith wasn't looking for a revolution. He was looking for a clean church. Born in 1927 under California's sun, raised in the rigid scaffolding of the Foursquare Gospel, Chuck was formed by a theology that knew the lines between sinner and saint, clean and unclean, saved and lost. He was a Bible man—one who trafficked in exposition and altar calls, not barefoot mystics or beachside baptisms. For two decades he pastored quiet churches tucked into the grid of the West,[37] holding fast to a vision of pastoral clarity, spiritual order, and a gospel that made sense—that is, of course, until the culture stopped making sense altogether.

"Chuck was a balding, personable man in his mid-forties with an infectious smile. He looked more like the traditional corner grocer."[38] He didn't understand the counterculture. He didn't *want* to. To him, the whole thing felt like a breakdown. Long hair, longer beards, bodies sprawled on sidewalks. "They're dirty," he once said. "They stink. They live in communes and sleep around. They take drugs and they're not interested in anything but themselves."[39] He would drive by the beaches of Huntington and Laguna and scoff at what he saw—young people unmoored, untethered, untamed. From the driver's seat of his car, *they* weren't lost sheep. They were rebels. Freaks. More in need of soap than salvation.[40]

But revival rarely checks with our judgemental categories before it begins. Sometimes, God moves through the back door of our certainties.

Kay Smith, Chuck's wife, saw it first. The same young people Chuck dismissed as spiritual detritus, Kay saw as beloved. "Chuck," she said, watching them wander the coastline like exiles, "these kids are lost. Somebody's got to reach them. Somebody has to tell them about Jesus."[41] Her tears became prayers. Her prayers became persistence. And eventually, Chuck's certainty gave way to curiosity. He started praying, hesitantly, for this alien generation he could neither comprehend nor trust.

That's when the door cracked open.

37. Vitello, "Chuck Smith," paras. 17–18
38. Enroth et al., *Jesus People*, 86.
39. Laurie and Vaughn, *Jesus Revolution*, 85.
40. Smith and Steven, *Reproducers*, 38.
41. Laurie and Vaughn, *Jesus Revolution*, 87.

Their daughter, Janette, had befriended a group of Christian hippies in Costa Mesa—a commune of barefoot Jesus freaks who worshiped with guitars and spoke in tongues. Through her, Chuck and Kay met John Higgins, one of the group's leaders. And through Higgins, they met Lonnie Frisbee.[42]

Lonnie was a paradox. A former acid head who claimed to have seen Christ while tripping on LSD in Tahquitz Canyon, he looked more like a rogue prophet than a respectable preacher.[43] Bearded, barefoot, burning with a kind of Spirit-fire that didn't come from seminaries or Sunday school. Kay saw it instantly. Chuck wasn't so sure. "He looked like John the Baptist in a sleeping bag," he later quipped.[44] Others described him as a long-haired, bearded Jesus-looking hippie Christian.[45] Either way, Kay insisted. She had seen the hunger.

It was sometime in early 1968, just after Lonnie's desert encounter, when the young preacher, sandals in hand, literally showed up on the Smiths' doorstep in Costa Mesa, or so the movie tells the story.[46] Not every telling remembers it the same way;[47] nonetheless, "The meeting was electric."[48] Lonnie stood there, shy and unannounced, a hitchhiking messiah with nothing but a Bible and a story about a vision of thousands craving baptism at the ocean's edge. Chuck described it like this, "One evening about 5 o'clock our doorbell rang. And there was a really honest to goodness hippie. Long hair, beard, flowers in his hair, bells on the cuffs of his pants, barefooted . . . and Lonnie extended his hand and there was such a warmth and love manifested in his greeting . . . I was caught off guard. There was an instant bond. There was a power of God's Spirit upon his life."[49]

That unplanned visit, the connection Janette begged for, moved Chuck. Not because of the theatrics, but because of the posture. Lonnie didn't demand the pulpit; he offered to wash trucks, plant gardens—anything to live out what he preached. Greg Laurie would later say that it was like

42. Laurie, "Long Strange Trip," para. 12.
43. Di Sabatino, dir., *Frisbee.*
44. Eskridge, "God's Forever Family," 125.
45. Bustraan, *Jesus People Movement*, 45.
46. Erwin and McCorkle, dirs., *Jesus Revolution.*
47. Laurie, "Jesus Revolution," para. 12.
48. Di Sabatino, dir., *Frisbee.*
49. Di Sabatino, dir., *Frisbee.*

"John Lennon met Paul McCartney or Steve Jobs met Steve Wozniak or when nitro met glycerin."[50] Chuck later admitted, "I was not at all prepared for the love that this young man would radiate."[51]

And in that raw encounter—no stage, no lights, no announcement—Chuck began to see a Spirit unfamiliar but undeniable. Something inside Chuck softened. Lonnie moved in. Literally, he moved in. And within a week about thirty-five more hippies found their way into the home of Chuck and Kay Smith as a new crashing pad. Lonnie and his wife, Connie, continued to stay with the Smiths, and soon Chuck's quiet tract home in Orange County became a spiritual boot camp for a Jesus revolution.[52]

And then came the night Chuck gave Lonnie the mic.

* * *

"Calvary Chapel has become a tourist attraction.
It's pastor has become a celebrity."[53]

* * *

The Mic . . . and Everything After

It started small.

There were maybe forty people in the small Calvary Chapel sanctuary. One barefoot preacher with a beard like the Galilean's and a heart full of thunder. It was 1968—a Wednesday night Bible study at the little Costa Mesa church.[54] Just another midweek service. And then Lonnie Frisbee opened his mouth and called down fire.

The sanctuary gathered its usual crowd—mothers with highlighted Bibles, men with loosened ties, teachers scribbling on notepads, maybe a few cynics lingering in the back.[55] And then the bells came. Not church bells. Not liturgical chimes. Anklet bells—bright, jangling, irreverent. Fifteen

50. Laurie and Vaughn, *Jesus Revolution*, 86–87.
51. Di Sabatino, dir., *Frisbee*.
52. Frisbee and Sachs, *Great Commission*, 68–71.
53. Enroth et al., *Jesus People*, 86–86.
54. Laurie and Vaughn, *Jesus Revolution*, 91.
55. Philpott, *Awakenings in America*, 90.

long-haired kids floated down the aisle wearing tie-dye and granny dresses, faded jeans and flowers in their hair. Barefoot. Bible-clutching. Beaming.[56]

There were plenty of open pews. They didn't care. They walked right past them and sat cross-legged on the floor beneath the pulpit.[57]

"There was a collective gasp from the pews, then silence in Calvary Chapel," Greg Laurie remembered. "Chuck looked at his congregation. His congregation looked at the hippies. The hippies smiled back, holding their new Bibles in their laps."[58]

That's how it started.

Not a campaign or a strategy. Not a branding effort or church growth plan. Like every true revival, it started in the margins—in the clash between what was expected and what was happening.

Lonnie had no credentials. No theological training. No sermon outlines or seminary polish. What he had was presence. Charisma. That raw, street-level electricity that made your skin hum. He looked like a prophet who'd wandered out of the desert—barefoot, bell-bottomed, sun-soaked, and still burning from that acid-fueled vision in Tahquitz Canyon, where he claimed he'd seen thousands waiting to be baptized in the Pacific.[59]

That first night wasn't smooth. It wasn't polished. But it was electric. The gospel didn't just get preached—it detonated.

Don Williams recalled Lonnie "slaughtering" the King James text, mangling verses, misreading passages—and somehow delivering one of the most powerful altar calls he'd ever seen.[60]

Oden Fong, himself a former member of the Brotherhood of Eternal Love, remembered him as "a horrible worship leader" who didn't know much of the Bible, but had "so much boldness and conviction . . . His message was

56. Laurie and Vaughn, *Jesus Revolution*, 91.

57. Philpott, *Awakenings in America*, 90.

58. Laurie and Vaughn, *Jesus Revolution*, 91–92.

59. Laurie, "Long Strange Trip," para. 10.

60. Eskridge, "God's Forever Family," 126.

very simple."[61] And yet, as he said, "anywhere he'd go he would draw people like he was a pied piper."[62]

Kent Philpott initially dismissed Lonnie as a nobody. "A weak personality," he said. Until he heard him speak. Over the years "he attracted hundreds, if not thousands . . . he looked like a picture of Jesus . . . I don't think I've seen that kind of power . . . it was incredible."[63]

Young David Rosales said it plainly: "He was a real hippie."[64] And maybe that's what made all the difference.

Greg Laurie once told the story of eating dinner at Lonnie's house before a service. Lonnie said he might preach on Jonah, asked Greg to read a few verses, and that was the entire prep. No notes. No manuscript. Just Jonah. But that night, Laurie watched as Lonnie preached those verses—"some of his facts weren't quite right," he admitted—but when the invitation came, dozens of kids streamed forward. The conclusion was inescapable: "Lonnie Frisbee might be the human instrument, but it was God who was at work here."[65]

Lonnie's power wasn't precision. It was presence.

And from that pulpit on that Wednesday night, something was born.

About forty people came that night. But within two years, in the summer of 1971, over a thousand—most under age twenty-one—were packing Calvary Chapel every Wednesday.[66] Not just Wednesdays, but the rest of the week as well. They ran out of pews. They sprawled across aisles. Some were high. Some were skeptical. Some were barefoot. But they came—because something about this gospel didn't smell like shame. It smelled like freedom.

At its height, Calvary was seeing 150 new converts every week. Chuck Smith reported that "upward of 500 young people a month are baptized."[67]

They added a second Sunday service. Then a third. The sanctuary technically held 425. The early services drew up to 500 each. The third often squeezed

61. Eskridge, "God's Forever Family," 73.
62. Eskridge, "God's Forever Family," 73.
63. Eskridge, "God's Forever Family," 73.
64. Eskridge, "God's Forever Family," 73.
65. Eskridge, "God's Forever Family," 74.
66. Enroth et al., *Jesus People*, 87.
67. Enroth et al., *Jesus People*, 86.

in 200 more than the fire code allowed. "The midweek Bible studies," one writer said, "were a fire marshal's nightmare"—but a Jesus Freak's dream.[68]

The Smiths took in so many barefoot believers that they bought a separate house—"The House of Miracles."[69] When that overflowed, they bought an old hotel. A trickle had become a flood. Calvary Chapel became the hub of something that couldn't be managed, only marveled at.[70]

Chuck Smith, for all his old-school Pentecostal instincts, certainly didn't buy in right away. He was cautious. Steady. Wary of wildfire. But his wife Kay saw it. She saw something radiant in Lonnie—and Chuck, trusting her discernment, took a holy risk.

He handed Lonnie the mic.

And that act—giving voice to the wild, unwashed, unschooled prophet—became the ignition spark.

What followed wasn't just revival. It was friction.

Church carpets buckled under the weight of dirty feet. Some longtime members bristled. One morning, a sign appeared at the sanctuary entrance to protect the newly installed carpet: "No Bare Feet Allowed in the Church." Chuck tore it down on sight.[71]

That same morning he told the board, if clean carpets mean turning away hungry souls, then rip up the carpet and bring in folding chairs. That was his line in the sand. The board backed him. A few old-timers walked. Most stayed. And the church embraced a no-reservations policy for the kingdom of God.[72] Revival over respectability. Spirit over system. Jesus over tradition.

By 1970, Calvary Chapel was hosting three Sunday services and drawing 1,500 a week. Pirate's Cove baptisms in the Pacific became iconic, just as in Lonnie's acid-induced vision. Orange County teens started trading joints for Bibles. Respectability took a backseat to transformation.[73]

68. Enroth et al., *Jesus People*, 86.
69. Smith, "Lonnie Frisbee," para. 5.
70. Frisbee and Sachs, *Great Commission*, 69–70.
71. Eskridge, "God's Forever Family," 75.
72. Eskridge, "God's Forever Family," 75–76.
73. Eskridge, "God's Forever Family," 76.

It was combustion.

By 1974, Calvary Chapel opened a new 2,300-seat auditorium—and within five weeks, they again needed triple services to contain the overflow.[74] The Spirit didn't just show up. It ran wild.

This was also the beginning of multiplication. Chuck Smith started releasing protégés to plant churches—one of whom, Kenn Gulliksen, would go on to help found the Vineyard movement.[75] The Calvary Chapel movement, born of the margins, now had tributaries.

But the memory that holds it all together—the crack in the veil, the birth of the fire—was that one Wednesday night.

When Chuck Smith, now reluctant patriarch of the Jesus Revolution, tore down a sign and opened the doors wide.

It began when Chuck gave Lonnie the mic.

* * *

"They like the goodies, but they hate me."
—Lonnie Frisbee[76]

* * *

End of an Era

But at the center of it all—at least in the beginning—was Lonnie.

He wasn't just charismatic. He was *liminal*—a figure suspended between worlds. He was a holy misfit who forced the church to ask deeper questions about who gets to speak, who gets to lead, and where the Spirit shows up.

Because here's the thing: Lonnie was never safe. Revival never is.

As Calvary Chapel institutionalized in the early 1970s, tensions mounted. Lonnie's free-flowing, charismatically expressive style, including healings, speaking in tongues, prophetic visions, and associations with faith leaders, began to feel out of step with Calvary's lean toward verse-by-verse

74. Bustraan, *Jesus People Movement*, 74.

75. Bustraan, *Jesus People Movement*, 75.

76. Di Sabatino, dir., *Frisbee.*

expository teaching.[77] Chuck Smith became increasingly concerned that the movement was veering into excess. In 1971, Smith started pulling back—discreetly but decisively. By late that year, Lonnie was asked to step down. The official narrative was that Lonnie and Connie needed time to focus on their marriage. But it was clear, Calvary was shifting, and Lonnie no longer fit its emerging mold.[78]

Some called it necessary. Others called it tragic. But all agreed—it was the end of an era.

Thus ended his first great season of influence—three brief, brilliant years.

Even so, the fire he lit didn't die.

End of a Marriage

Their marriage was ignited in the wildfire optimism of Jesus People idealism. It was 1968, and they were shoulder to shoulder with other barefoot believers in the Big House commune—a half-mission, half-chaos collision of radical hospitality and raw, unfiltered faith. But that kind of spiritual intensity doesn't always translate into healthy rhythms. Revival doesn't come with a rule book. Lonnie was always moving—preaching, praying, chasing the Spirit. And Connie? More and more, she was left behind.[79]

"He didn't know how to be a husband," she would later say. "He only knew how to be a preacher."[80] And Lonnie—driven by calling, haunted by the past—never really stopped running. Ministry, especially revival ministry, can be intoxicating. The applause. The spiritual high. The adrenaline. But beneath all that, his wounds remained untouched. He hadn't found healing. He'd just found a stage.

In 1972, they moved to Florida to join the authoritarian Shepherding Movement under Bob Mumford. The promise was order, structure, covering, and submission. Maybe it would hold him. Maybe it would heal him. It didn't. Though Frisbee flourished briefly, traveling as a missionary,

77. Di Sabatino, dir., *Frisbee*.

78. Adams, "Generation Led to Jesus," 13.

79. Salter, "Lonnie Frisbee."

80. Di Sabatino, dir., *Frisbee*.

preaching overseas, it couldn't reach what was fractured within.[81] By 1973, the marriage unraveled. They divorced that year. Lonnie was only twenty-three, a divorced prophet without a parish, still carrying too much fire and no container to hold it.[82]

Connie, with grace and grit, later said he lacked the "balanced mentoring" and accountability he so desperately needed.[83] The church, for all its revival rhetoric, had no framework for someone like him—not for his level of giftedness, nor for the depth of his brokenness. So Lonnie drifted.

By the late 1970s, he returned to Southern California. Quieter. Chastened. But the Spirit? The Spirit wasn't done with him yet.

Vineyard

It was Mother's Day, 1980, Calvary Chapel, Yorba Linda, California at John Wimber's church. The church was one of the Calvary Chapel church plants birthed from the growth Lonnie Frisbee ignited in his time in Costa Mesa. It was still under the Calvary Chapel umbrella and it was hosting guest preacher Lonnie Frisbee.[84]

What happened that night is now Jesus Movement lore.

Lonnie gave a short message about the Holy Spirit. He prayed. And then the room broke open. Teens fell to their knees, weeping. Others spoke in tongues. The air was electric with divine encounter. "It was like Acts chapter 2," Wimber later recalled.[85]

This wasn't church growth. It was a spiritual combustion. The next weeks saw the congregation explode with hunger for God. Healings. Deliverance. More conversions. Wimber's quiet Calvary Chapel church plant became the seedbed for what would become the Vineyard Movement.[86]

But such a Spirit-fueled eruption created tension with Chuck Smith and the more restrained Calvary leadership. Just two years later, in 1982, Smith gave

81. Salter, "Lonnie Frisbee."

82. Smith, "Lonnie Frisbee," para. 6.

83. Salter, "Lonnie Frisbee," para. 17.

84. Frisbee and Sachs, *Great Commission*, 137.

85. Frisbee and Sachs, *Great Commission*, 153–54.

86. Frisbee and Sachs, *Great Commission*, 138–40.

Wimber and several churches his blessing to officially part ways and form a new association: the Vineyard Fellowship.[87] It included eight churches originally planted by Kenn Gulliksen, a former Lutheran[88] and the lesser-known but true founder of the Vineyard name.[89] While Wimber became the movement's primary face, both he and Gulliksen would credit Lonnie's Mother's Day sermon as the spark that lit the fire.

It was his second major role in launching a global church-planting movement. How big of a movement? Well, today the Vineyard website states that "130,000 people call about 500 churches home throughout the United States."[90]

He was barely in his thirties.

And once again, for Lonnie, it didn't last.

* * *

"'How do you know Lonnie is a homosexual?
Has he told you himself?' I said, 'Yes. He has.'"
—Chuck Smith Jr.[91]

* * *

Outcast

It's one of the great ironies—and tragedies—of the Jesus Movement: the man whose barefoot preaching lit the match of revival was later rejected by the very institutions that caught fire from his witness. Lonnie Frisbee was no stranger to contradiction. He called down the Holy Spirit like thunder, yet carried a secret the church wasn't ready to hold. The secret? Homosexuality.

David Di Sabatino, who documented Lonnie's life with sensitivity and honesty, recalled, "His early testimony at Calvary Chapel was that he had come out of the homosexual lifestyle, but he felt like a leper because a lot of people turned away from him after that . . . and I think that's an indictment

87. Eskridge, "God's Forever Family," 265.
88. Di Sabatino, dir., *Frisbee.*
89. Frisbee and Sachs, *Great Commission*, 191, 206.
90. Vineyard USA, "Growing Community of Local Churches."
91. Di Sabatino, dir., *Frisbee.*

of the church."[92] In another moment, he told Lonnie's family the painful truth: "He defined himself as gay, way back. Nobody knew that."[93]

And yet, Lonnie himself later insisted, "I have never even considered myself a homosexual at all . . . I never lived the gay lifestyle," instead naming his experiences as moments of confusion and trauma, molestation, rebellion, and backsliding, not identity.[94] Still, the church—first Calvary Chapel, then Vineyard—released him. Not for theological error, not for lack of fruit, but for being too human in what was, in their opinion, the wrong way.

And so the man who helped ignite two of the most significant revivals in modern church history died on the margins of the very movement he helped birth. That isn't just sad—it's a caution. If the Spirit descends through the outsider, the wounded, the "unqualified," then God help us when we dismiss the one who bleeds.

Somewhere in the 1980s, Lonnie contracted HIV. He never said exactly how. But those close to him assumed it came from a same-sex encounter.[95] AIDS was a death sentence then—and a social stigma of epic proportions. For a while, he told no one. He tried to pray it away. He asked God for healing. He withdrew further. But as the disease progressed, the symptoms became impossible to hide. Friends say he lost weight rapidly and became visibly ill by 1992.[96]

To his credit, Lonnie did not run from the end. He made peace with his past. He reconnected with old friends. At the end, Pastor John Wimber of Vineyard admitted that "Lonnie has contributed a lot to the church," and then offered any and all funds of Vineyard Ministry International to help with the costs of Lonnie's AIDS treatments. "Give him whatever he needs . . . if he needs a car or an apartment or food and utilities, Vineyard Ministries International will cover it."[97]

92. Chattaway, "Documentary of a Hippie Preacher," para. 15.
93. Chattaway, "Documentary of a Hippie Preacher," para. 13.
94. Frisbee and Sachs, *Great Commission*, 245.
95. Di Sabatino, dir., *Frisbee*.
96. Frisbee and Sachs, *Set Free*, 221.
97. Frisbee and Sachs, *Set Free*, 236.

Lonnie Frisbee died on March 12, 1993, of AIDS-related complications. He was forty-three. His funeral at the Crystal Cathedral drew hundreds. Chuck Smith gave the eulogy.

Frisbee's tombstone bears the verse from Zechariah 4:6 that he often quoted, "Not by might, nor by power, but by My Spirit, says the Lord."[98]

Lonnie Frisbee's life is hard to summarize because it wasn't a story—it was a rupture. From the start, it defied categories: a broken boy with a preacher's fire, an acid-tripping mystic who met Jesus in the canyons. Not in a church. Not in a revival tent. But on LSD, naked and hallucinating under desert stars.

And that's the point we often miss.

For all our discomfort, psychedelics weren't just recreational for Lonnie and the early Jesus People. They were revelatory. Or at least, they *seemed* to be. LSD wasn't the destination—but it cracked open the veil. It disoriented just enough to make space for Spirit. It disrupted long enough for Jesus to appear. These weren't just kids getting high. They were pilgrims looking for heaven in a world that had lost its shape.

And for a moment, it worked. The Spirit rushed in. People got saved. Churches exploded. Calvary Chapel went from a handful of souls to nearly a thousand churches in the United States, with hundreds more worldwide.[99] The Vineyard emerged like a second wave, now home to over 130,000 people across the country and 2,500 churches around the world.[100]

Lonnie stood at the center of it—sometimes leading, sometimes bleeding—but never irrelevant. He called down fire at Calvary, sparked revival at Vineyard, and baptized thousands in Pirate's Cove.[101] But the institutions couldn't hold him. His sexuality and his scars became too heavy for the systems he helped build. He was an outsider. He was the definition of the place the faithful choose not to look.

And yet . . . something lingered. Something that wasn't Lonnie but came through him or at least *because* of him.

98. Di Sabatino, dir., *Frisbee*.

99. Eskridge, "God's Forever Family," 216.

100. Vineyard Churches, "Vineyard Churches."

101. Smith and Steven, *Reproducers*, 39–42.

The music.

The revolution may have started in a psychedelic haze, but it stayed alive in the songs. Music was the language of a generation without maps. It carried the ache. The hope. The vision. It came from that same altered space—minor chords, suspended harmonies, lyrics that felt like prophecy. And while the church debated what to do with Frisbee, the music moved on without permission.

To be clear: what you've just read is a sliver. One shaft of light refracted through a cracked window named Lonnie. The Jesus Movement was bigger than him—but through him, we can see how LSD, music, and Spirit braided into something divine. Or at least . . . it *seemed* divine.

Lonnie died in 1993. But the music still plays.

And that's where the real mystery begins.

Not with a sermon.

But with a song born in the fog of vision.

Chapter 4

In the Beginning . . . the Birth of CCM

"Rock 'n' roll is everybody's fucking music . . . it's not just the devil's music. I think that's where God and the devil shake hands—right there."

—Neil Young[1]

Sound.

Sound is the word we give to that which we hear.

Okay. Okay. Technically, sound is a vibration that propagates as an acoustic wave through a transmission medium such as a gas, liquid, or solid. In human physiology and psychology, sound is the reception of such waves and the brain's perception of them.[2]

But we all know it is much more than that. Sound allows us to receive alerts, monitor surroundings, and—when mixed with some manipulation using a tongue, lips, and mouth—communicate with other people.

It's miraculous, really.

Which might be why the book of Genesis starts by letting us know that creation itself begins with sound—when God said, "Let there be light."[3]

1. McDonough, *Shakey*, 54.
2. Wikipedia, "Sound," para. 1.
3. Genesis 1:3.

It isn't a small thing. I mean, if there is a God that created all things, a God that is omnipotent and omnipresent, couldn't that God have simply *thought* creation into existence? Probably. But that isn't what happened.

God *spoke*.

And let's be honest—there is no "sound" in a void because there is no medium through which to transmit the vibration. That alone may make the ancient story even more powerful: sound itself has the power to create. It has the ability to propagate a wave, to send energy rippling through time and space. Lauren Daigle said of the sound of music, "It was a vehicle for me to see the richness of hope land upon someone's spirit . . . Rhythm, Rhyme, Melody . . . Sound . . . I don't understand it."[4]

And that is exactly how the sound of music operated in the midst of the counterculture.

LSD had a role in Lonnie's movement toward preaching the gospel. Lonnie had a role in that same gospel making its way to a bunch of musical hippies. The miraculous sound of the music made by those hippies is what carried it forward . . . but not just any music . . .

. . . Jesus Music.

Somehow, that music born in the counterculture of the 1960s and 1970s has become a multibillion-dollar industry today[5] . . . and it is growing—fast. Driven mostly by young people, the industry known as CCM (Contemporary Christian Music) has grown by about 60 percent between 2019 to 2024 alone.[6]

What does this look like, day in and day out, in everyday life in America? Well . . . every single morning, nearly 50 million people wake up and are inspired by the music first birthed out of LSD, Lonnie Frisbee, Chuck Smith, and Calvary Chapel.[7]

Fifty million!

Now that's a movement!

4. Erwin and Erwin, dirs., *Jesus Music.*
5. Erwin and Erwin, dirs., *Jesus Music.*
6. Madden, "Christian Music Is Experiencing," para. 2.
7. Erwin and Erwin, dirs., *Jesus Music.*

Devil Music

* * *

"The devil should not be allowed to keep
all the best tunes for himself."
—Martin Luther[8]

* * *

If sound has power, then it can't be neutral. That was the fear. Rock was labeled "the devil's music,"[9] a sonic battleground where gospel and temptation collided. There were historical echoes here: Martin Luther once wrote that *music is hated by the devil* because it drives him away as surely as Scripture does.[10] The conviction was clear—if music carried weight, it could pull heavenward or drag toward hell.

By the late 1960s and early 1970s, this fear became a rallying cry. Larry Norman picked it up and hurled it back at the critics. On *Only Visiting This Planet*, he sang it straight, "Why should the devil have all the good music?"[11] For him, rock wasn't the enemy.

It was raw material. Waiting to be reclaimed. Reframed. Sanctified.

But here's the thing—God has a long history of showing up where people least expect. The label "devil's music" may have been meant as a curse, but it was also a sign. A reminder that the Spirit often slips in through the cracks—into the sounds, the scenes, and the spaces the church is quickest to reject. When the center shouts "unholy," the edges become the very place where holiness erupts.

What had once been condemned as the devil's music was now being sanctified, turned into the language of evangelism.[12] For many, the accusation of being "too worldly" became its own proof—evidence that God was breaking in, using the sound of culture as a vessel.[13]

8. Madden, "Christian Music Is Experiencing," para 11.
9. Thornbury, *Why Should the Devil Have All the Good Music?*, 51–52.
10. Schäufele, "Martin Luther's Occasional Writings."
11. Norman, *Only Visiting This Planet.*
12. Stephens, *Devil's Music*, 178.
13. Payne, *God Gave Rock and Roll to You*, 114–16.

That has always been the scandal of incarnation. God showing up at the fringe. God moving at the edges of culture rather than at its safe, guarded center. And now—through rock 'n' roll. The very charge that guitars and drumbeats were profane became the backdrop against which the Spirit moved. What the church was quickest to dismiss, God was already using to sing people awake.

So when Calvary Chapel opened its doors to guitars and harmonies, it wasn't just a musical choice. It was a declaration. The sound that once shook dance halls could shake the sanctuary too—and in doing so, expose that the devil never owned the music in the first place.[14]

The Moment

* * *

> "I saw Contemporary Christian Music
> born right before my very eyes."
> —Greg Laurie[15]

* * *

Let me be clear. What happened at Calvary wasn't the beginning of Christian rock 'n' roll. The sound had already been stirring for years—an underground hum, low frequencies rattling the floorboards, waiting to break into resonance. But when that Christian music created with guitars and drums made its way into Christian culture—made its way into the sanctuary—that was the moment that still reverberates to this day . . . and clearly is getting louder and louder.

So—before Maranatha!, before Chuck Smith, before Lonnie, and before Love Song . . .

Before an acoustic guitar ever rang out inside Calvary Chapel, the ground was already trembling. "Christian rock" did not arrive ex nihilo in Costa Mesa. By the late 1960s, the fusion of faith and popular music had been bubbling under the surface for years. Evangelicals had long harnessed the power of popular song, from Southern gospel harmonizers and Elvis

14. Payne, *God Gave Rock and Roll to You*, 26–30.

15. Erwin and Erwin, dirs., *Jesus Music*.

influencers like the Blackwood Brothers and the Stamps Quartet, to revival choruses that stretched toward folk and even fuzzed-out garage rock.[16]

And then came the names.

> Larry Norman. Marsha Stevens. Andraé Crouch and the Disciples. Mylon LeFevre.
>
> Children of the Day. Agape.
>
> 2nd Chapter of Acts. Daniel Amos. Randy Matthews. Resurrection Band.
>
> The Archers. Randy Stonehill.[17]

A roll call. A groundswell. Not a genre with a single progenitor, but a movement—a collective of young voices rising from the ferment of late 1960s culture. Sex, drugs, rock and roll, and a gnawing spiritual hunger. Out of that mix came this music.

Some—like Norman[18] or Crouch[19]—carried the imprint of Pentecostal or Baptist roots. Others—like Keith and Melody Green—had little connection to American Christianity's gospel traditions. But all of them were chasing the same thing.[20] Each one tested the edges of what church music could sound like, even while critics dismissed it all as the devil's music.[21]

So when Love Song arrived at Calvary, they weren't inventing something new. They were amplifying a sound already rumbling underground—and transforming it into the anthem of a movement.

But their entry into Calvary Chapel's life wasn't automatic. Chuck Smith had grown up Pentecostal and was cautious about letting the trappings of the counterculture into his church. Still, he had also opened his pulpit to Lonnie Frisbee, the hippie-turned-evangelist who drew crowds of young people . . . and who soon caught the attention of a fledgling band called Love Song.

16. Stephens, *Devil's Music*, 42.
17. Payne, *God Gave Rock and Roll to You*, 40–41.
18. Payne, *God Gave Rock and Roll to You*, 38.
19. Stone, "Carman, Beloved by '90s Evangelical Kids," para. 5.
20. Payne, *God Gave Rock and Roll to You*, 41.
21. Payne, *God Gave Rock and Roll to You*, 26–30.

The band was made up of long-haired seekers who had already ridden the highs and lows of the California counterculture. They weren't outsiders looking in—they had lived it.

Chuck Girard of Love Song said it bluntly, "My philosophy was that God had given us LSD and that if you weren't brave enough to experiment with drugs, that you'd miss God because I thought that was the secret key."[22] Glenn Kaiser of Resurrection Band told his own version, "I literally took a spice rack off a wall one night and rolled a joint out of everything on the rack. I guarantee that you cannot even begin to get a buzz off any of that stuff. I tried."[23]

Still restless. Still reaching.

Then they heard about a place. Calvary Chapel. And they heard about a name.

Jesus.

Tommy Coomes of Love Song summed it up, "We had two great loves: the love of making music and this really driving urge to find out who God was."[24]

And so they went to Chuck Smith—guitars in hand. No doctrinal statements. No creeds. Just songs.

They played. Smith listened. And though not known as an emotional man, some recall that when Love Song performed, his eyes may have welled.[25]

The song was "Welcome Back." When it ended, Smith simply asked: "Can you play tonight? It's Youth Night. Lonnie's preaching."[26]

They said yes.

That night the sanctuary—normally home to a few dozen congregants—swelled with hundreds of young people.

22. Erwin and Erwin, dirs., *Jesus Music.*

23. Erwin and Erwin, dirs., *Jesus Music.*

24. Erwin and Erwin, dirs., *Jesus Music.*

25. Cloud, "Calvary Chapel and Maranatha Music," paras. 6–7.

26. Erwin and Erwin, dirs., *Jesus Music.*

What they heard was unlike anything a sanctuary had experienced before: folk-rock harmonies bent heavenward. Songs that sounded familiar in form but strange in address.

Chuck Girard reminded, "You gotta remember, up to that point, what was church music? Hymn book. Choir. Organ."[27]

This wasn't entertainment. It was worship—carried on the wings of guitars and harmony.

According to Greg Laurie, the songs were "about four chords. Simple lyrics, repeated again and again. In spite of the simplicity—or maybe because of it—the songs intrigued me. The kids weren't singing for themselves; it seemed like they were singing to someone."[28]

That verticality—lyrics rising instead of circling inward—turned simple songs into worship, not performance.

Within months, Calvary had exploded with new converts, baptisms, and musicians. In less than six months, a dozen or more bands were playing weekly.[29]

What began as a handful of hippies singing testimonies quickly became one of the first serious Christian labels for the new genre.

But at the center were the songs themselves. Many in the congregation experienced Love Song's music sacramentally: "Many felt that God was made present through the strumming guitars and sweet harmonies of Love Song and 2nd Chapter of Acts."[30]

That is why the first Youth Night with Love Song mattered. It wasn't just a concert. It was an encounter. A mediation of God through harmony and acoustic strings. A sacrament.

Looking back, what set this moment apart was that these young bands weren't trying to launch an industry. They didn't even know one was possible. "In the beginning, we didn't know there was a movement."[31]

27. Erwin and Erwin, dirs., *Jesus Music.*
28. Eskridge, "God's Forever Family," 72.
29. Erwin and Erwin, dirs., *Jesus Music.*
30. Payne, *God Gave Rock and Roll to You*, 42.
31. Erwin and Erwin, dirs., *Jesus Music.*

They were simply trying to connect their generation's sounds with their newfound faith. "For us, we just continued the same music that we loved with a whole different heart and attitude."[32]

That night at Calvary Chapel was just a band of hippies daring to sing Jesus into their own idiom—and a pastor crazy enough to let it happen.

The industry? That came later.

But the floodgates opened. Calvary Chapel had become a breeding ground for music. Guitars and harmonies were no longer intrusions; they were the pulse of revival.

Bands sprouted fast—names that still echo in Jesus Music lore: Children of the Day, whose ballad "For Those Tears I Died" became an early anthem;[33] as well as Country Faith, Daniel Amos, Chuck Girard, Karen Lafferty, and The Way.[34] By 1971, Chuck Smith recognized the need to capture it. He launched Maranatha! Music—not with industry ambition, but to preserve what was happening on Saturday nights in Costa Mesa.[35]

The first album was *The Everlastin' Living Jesus Music Concert* in 1971. Plain white cover. Red dove in the center.[36] Remember that—it comes back.

In future recordings, simple, Scripture-based songs such as "Father, I Adore You" (1972),[37] "Seek Ye First" (1972),[38] and "Humble Thyself in the Sight of the Lord" (1978)[39] gave voice to a new way of praying together in song.

These choruses—often written on the fly, sung in living rooms and coffeehouses—became the seedbed of Contemporary Christian Music, which then turned into what would be called praise and worship music.

At first, it was a constellation of voices, each orbiting around Calvary. But in the firmament of Jesus Music, one star burned brighter—and stranger—than all the rest.

32. Erwin and Erwin, dirs., *Jesus Music.*
33. Payne, *God Gave Rock and Roll to You*, 51.
34. Rabey, "Maranatha! Music Turns Twenty," 12.
35. Thornbury, *Why Should the Devil Have All the Good Music?*, 67–68.
36. Various Artists, *Everlastin' Living Jesus Music Concert.*
37. Coelho, *Father, I Adore You.*
38. Lafferty, *Seek Ye First the Kingdom of God.*
39. Hudson, *Humble Thyself in the Sight of the Lord.*

Larry Norman

Larry Norman is probably the most amazing artists you've never heard of.[40] If Love Song was the house band of Jesus Music, then Larry Norman was its lightning rod. Restless. Theatrical. Unsettling. He turned rock into an altar call and made the church blush in the process. Norman didn't just write songs. He staged collisions between gospel and counterculture that nobody could ignore. Many consider him to be "the single most important figure in Christian rock."[41]

From the start, he refused to cede the soundscape. "Why should the devil have all the good music?" became his rallying cry—less a question than a gauntlet. He was convinced rock was not Satan's possession but God's creation.[42]

His 1972 album *Only Visiting This Planet* made that defiance explicit.[43] Norman didn't soften the edges or sanitize the riffs. He baptized them. The record played like a liturgy for the counterculture: electric guitars, biting satire, and lyrics that named Vietnam, racism, drugs, and hypocrisy alongside salvation and resurrection.

He wrote the kind of lyrics that would never find their way onto a *Christian* album today. From his song "Why Don't You Look Into Jesus"[44] he writes lines such as,

> Sipping whiskey from a paper cup.
> You drown your sorrows 'til you can't stand up
> and, Gonorrhea on Valentine's Day
> And you're still looking for the perfect lay and,
> Shooting junk 'til you're half insane.
> A broken needle in your purple vein.

Even earlier, in 1970, Norman wrote "No More LSD For Me"—a song that memorialized the journey from psychedelics to Jesus Music. It was a

40. Joseph, "RIP: Larry Norman," para. 1.
41. Erwin and Erwin, dirs., *Jesus Music.*
42. Stephens, *Devil's Music*, 180.
43. Thornbury, *Why Should the Devil Have All the Good Music?*, 80.
44. Norman, "Why Don't You Look Into Jesus?," on *Only Visiting This Planet.*

cultural pivot pressed into three minutes of vinyl: "No more LSD for me, I met a man from Galilee."[45]

Rock, for many evangelicals, was still coded as dangerous and Larry leaned into that . . . hard. However, his son remembers that Norman believed that reclaiming rock 'n' roll for the church was his mission.[46] To some, the beat itself was demonic. Norman leaned into that suspicion, standing at the crossroads and daring the church to see God moving there. He embodied the paradox of Jesus Music: at once insider and outsider, confessing faith while wielding the very cultural tools evangelicals feared. He was "too Christian for the secular world and too secular for the Christian world."[47]

Norman was not interested in making worship choruses or safe singalongs. His lyrics were prophecy more than praise. On *Reader's Digest,* he blasted American politics, corporate greed, and religious hypocrisy.[48] In *The Great American Novel,* he lamented racism and war while pointing to Jesus as the only hope.[49] These weren't Sunday morning hymns. They were street sermons with guitar solos.

The reality is that Larry was a difficult person.[50] The church thought him too brash. The industry too religious. Audiences unsure. He was a man without a country, caught between two worlds—too Christian for the counterculture, too countercultural for Christians.

That tension was his genius. He refused to give either side the clean lines it wanted.

Where Love Song invited hippies into the sanctuary, Norman dragged the sanctuary into the streets. His stage presence—long blonde hair, sharp humor, piercing gaze—was itself a sign. He looked like a rock star. Sounded like a prophet. Sang like a man convinced the headlines were apocalyptic.

His legacy was messy but seismic. Without Norman, the ground Love Song stood on might never have been cleared. His insistence that rock belonged to God cracked open the door that others—Michael W. Smith, Stryper,

45. Norman, "No More LSD For Me," on *Street Level.*

46. Erwin and Erwin, dirs., *Jesus Music.*

47. Erwin and Erwin, dirs., *Jesus Music.*

48. Norman, *Reader's Digest.*

49. Norman, *Great American Novel.*

50. Payne, *God Gave Rock and Roll to You,* 170.

Petra, Amy Grant, DC Talk—would later walk through. But in his own time, Norman remained on the threshold. Guitar in hand. Declaring the devil never owned the music in the first place.

Explo '72

* * *

"When you play at about 140db, they either listen or they leave."
—Glenn Kaiser, Resurrection Band (*The Jesus Music*)[51]

* * *

Billboards went up across Dallas. Full-page ads shouted: "Something historic is going to happen here."[52]

And happen it did.

Riding the wave of the Jesus Revolution, Campus Crusade for Christ's International Student Congress on Evangelism—better known as Explo '72, short for *Spiritual Explosion*[53]—erupted into Dallas as the largest youth training conference in church history.[54]

Billy Graham called it a "religious Woodstock."[55] Others said it was a children's crusade. A Texas-sized happening. Whatever the label, the scale was staggering.

It was the biggest Jesus Music festival anyone had ever seen. The *New York Times* reported an attendance of 75,000.[56] But, police and newspapers counted 120,000 to 180,000.[57] Either way, the numbers thundered.

What happened there was more than a rally. It was a retuning of sound and symbol. The lineup blurred lines—white Jesus Music voices like Larry Norman, Randy Mathews, and Love Song sharing the stage with Black

51. Erwin and Erwin, dirs., *Jesus Music*.
52. Plowman, "Explo '72," para. 1.
53. Turner, "Explo '72," paras. 1–2.
54. Plowman, "Explo '72," para. 1.
55. Fiske, "'Religious Woodstock' Draws 75,000," para. 1.
56. Fiske, "'Religious Woodstock' Draws 75,000," para. 3.
57. Plowman, "Explo '72," para. 1.

Gospel powerhouses Willa Dorsey and Andraé Crouch & the Disciples, alongside country royalty like Connie Smith and Johnny Cash. It was church and counterculture, gospel choir and rock band, denim and rhinestones—all on one platform. Campus Crusade captured it in a double album called *Jesus Sound Explosion,* a vinyl artifact that froze the moment when sacred and secular collided, pressed together into grooves that testified revival could come dressed in any sound.[58]

Graham supplied the gravitas—but the magnet was the music. Youth came not for pageantry but for the pulse—for the jeans-and-sideburns Jesus rockers who made faith sound like their lives. A *Life* magazine cover marveled at the order and kindness,[59] while on stage Johnny Cash testified saying, "I have tried drugs and a little of everything else, and there is nothing in the world more satisfying than having the kingdom of God building inside of you and growing."[60] In pop culture terms, the Jesus Movement had arrived.

Explo '72 condensed a broader shift: disparate streams—Southern Gospel, Black Gospel, Jesus music—sharing one platform to call for Jesus. And in that moment, the center of gravity moved. Billy Graham wasn't the main draw. The bands were. The sanctuary hadn't just welcomed guitars—America's youth had cranked up the volume on the Great Commission.

Call it a hinge in the story: stadium-scale youth, Billy Graham's imprimatur, and a soundtrack that refused to cede the airwaves. After Dallas, no one could pretend Jesus Music was a sideshow. It *was* the show.

LSD. Hippies. Lonnie. Chuck. Jesus Movement. The Seventies. Jesus Music.

And next—the sound shifts again. From Jesus Music to Contemporary Christian Music. From counterculture choruses to CCM.

58. Various Artists, *Jesus Sound Explosion.*

59. *Life*, "Great Jesus Rally in Dallas," cover.

60. Thornbury, *Why Should the Devil Have All the Good Music?*, 75.

Amy Grant

* * *

"I was 14 and I just heard this very acoustic music and they had 'Jesus' lyrics . . . and I loved it."
—Amy Grant[61]

* * *

By the late 1970s, Contemporary Christian Music was beginning to find its voice, but it was Amy Grant who gave it a face. Her self-titled debut in 1977 introduced her as a teenager with a guitar and an open faith. Grant had first been drawn in at the Koinonia Coffeehouse in Nashville, where she heard "Jesus lyrics" sung over the acoustic strum of guitars. It was a sonic connection to the Jesus People—a sound that carried the same wave of hope she had only felt before in worship.[62] Two years later, her album *My Father's Eyes* climbed to the top of *Billboard*'s Inspirational LPs chart,[63] and soon she was opening Billy Graham crusades with the Bill Gaither Trio.[64] With her bright smile and unthreatening presence, Grant embodied what evangelicals wanted to project: faith packaged in a form suburban America could embrace.

The breakthrough came in 1982 with *Age to Age*, the first Contemporary Christian album ever to go platinum.[65] Songs like "El Shaddai" and "Sing Your Praise to the Lord" carried the intimacy of Jesus Music but with polished pop production that made them instantly accessible. It was the sound of revival repackaged for FM radio. By the mid-1980s, Grant was no longer just a church favorite; she was a cultural phenomenon. Her 1984 Grammy-winning song "Angels" played like an evangelical response to MTV.[66]

Then came the leap. In 1991, *Heart in Motion* catapulted her fully into the mainstream with "Baby, Baby" and "Every Heartbeat," songs that topped *Billboard* charts and sold millions.[67] To some, this was victory: proof that

61. Erwin and Erwin, dirs., *Jesus Music*.
62. Payne, *God Gave Rock and Roll to You*, 55.
63. "Grammy Awards 1980."
64. Payne, *God Gave Rock and Roll to You*, 61.
65. "Evening with Amy Grant."
66. Grammy Awards, "Amy Grant Wins Best Gospel Performance, Female."
67. Payne, *God Gave Rock and Roll to You*, 89.

Christian music could hold its own alongside Madonna and Whitney Houston. To others, it felt like betrayal. Grant danced and flirted in a video with a man who wasn't her husband, and evangelical bookstores refused to stock the album. The tension was clear: Was she a pop star who sang about Jesus, or a Christian artist dabbling in pop?

But controversy didn't slow her down. *Heart in Motion* sold more than five million copies,[68] breaking every ceiling that CCM had ever known. Evangelical tastemakers reframed her mainstream visibility as legitimization, a sign that their values had crossed into national consciousness. For industry leaders, the numbers were almost sacramental—700,000 records meant, in their rhetoric, 700,000 souls reached.[69]

But . . .

Her personal life only fueled the scrutiny. In 1999, Grant divorced her husband, Gary Chapman, and later married country singer Vince Gill. For evangelicals, divorce was still a scandal, and her private pain became public fodder. Critics wondered if she had abandoned her roots. Fans countered that her honesty made her more human, more relatable, more real. Either way, her place in music history was secure.[70]

Grant's career traced the arc of the industry itself: from coffeehouse choruses to platinum records, from Christian bookstores to Top 40 radio, from revival tents to MTV. Where earlier pioneers fought from the margins, Grant carried the sound into the mainstream. Or did the sound from the Jesus People who were part of the Jesus Movement singing Jesus Music carry her forward?

The numbers speak. More than 30 million albums sold. One billion global streams. Six Grammy Awards. Over twenty-six Dove Awards. She was the first Christian artist to earn a platinum record, the first to earn a double-platinum, the first to take Christian music onto the pop charts and stay there.[71]

Her critics asked whether she had gone too far. Her career answered with another question: What if going too far was exactly the point—proof that the gospel could live on the airwaves of Top 40 radio?

68. RIAA, "Gold & Platinum."
69. Payne, *God Gave Rock and Roll to You*, 90.
70. Payne, *God Gave Rock and Roll to You*, 100.
71. The Factory, "Amy Grant."

But Amy Grant wasn't alone. Alongside her rise stood a young keyboard player and songwriter named Michael W. Smith. First as her collaborator and then as a solo artist, Smith's soaring ballads and worship anthems would carry CCM from concert halls to church pews, from pop radio to global praise.

Michael W. Smith

* * *

"The music I loved was the Beatles, Elton John, Billy Joel."
—Michael W. Smith[72]

* * *

If Amy Grant gave CCM its face, Michael W. Smith gave it its soundtrack.

By the early 1980s, his story had already intertwined with Amy Grant's. In 1981, he signed with Meadowgreen Music, penning songs for Sandi Patty, Kathy Troccoli, Bill Gaither—and Grant herself. A year later, he joined her Age to Age tour as a keyboardist. Soon he was her opening act.[73] By 1983, he released his debut, *The Michael W. Smith Project,* with the now-classic "Friends," co-written with his wife Deborah.[74] It became an anthem—sung at graduations, youth rallies, funerals. The soundtrack of evangelical friendship. By the mid-1980s, Smith wasn't just backing Amy Grant—he was carrying his own spotlight.

And he did more than carry it. He ran with it.

In 1990 came *Go West Young Man*[75] and the crossover hit "Place in This World," which debuted on the *Billboard* Hot 100 at number six.[76] Suddenly a Christian songwriter from West Virginia was on the same charts as Madonna and Mariah. Two years later, *Change Your World*[77] dropped,

72. Erwin and Erwin, dirs., *Jesus Music.*
73. Erickson, "Michael W. Smith," para 19.
74. Smith, *Michael W. Smith Project.*
75. Smith, *Go West Young Man.*
76. *Billboard,* "Michael W. Smith."
77. Smith, *Change Your World.*

with "I Will Be Here for You" topping the Adult Contemporary charts.[78] By the early 1990s, Smith was no longer the apprentice—he was the keeper of CCM's canon.

To date, he has earned three Grammys, forty-five Dove Awards, and sold almost twenty million albums.

He had arrived.

But the spark? The origin? The moment when it all started?

That wasn't on stage. Not in a studio. Not on tour with Amy Grant.

It was in a thrift store record bin.

A white cover. A red dove. *The Everlasting Living Jesus Music Concert.*

Michael W. Smith picked it up. Flipped it over. Saw that every single song was about Jesus. And he knew. "That's what I want to do."[79]

Whether he realized it or not, that vinyl was more than music. It was inheritance. A line back to Calvary Chapel, to Chuck Smith, to Lonnie Frisbee pulling stoned hippies into baptismal waters. And further still—back to the psychedelic soil that cracked open the church and let sound rush in.

Michael W. Smith heard the echo. And he decided to join the song.

In 2001, Michael W. Smith started hearing a voice.

"For such a time as this."[80]

He ignored it. Brushed it off. Ran from it. Hid from it. The words haunted him. He thought maybe it meant a worship album. He didn't want to do it. He wasn't ready. He had built his career on pop, on CCM, on carrying the gospel into the charts. Worship felt like retreat.

Three weeks later the voice came back.

"For such a time as this."

So he stopped running. He called in every big name from the CCM world. He wrote. He arranged. He recorded. And what came out wasn't a retreat. It

78. *Billboard*, "Adult Contemporary Music Chart."

79. Erwin and Erwin, dirs., *Jesus Music.*

80. Erwin and Erwin, dirs., *Jesus Music.*

was an explosion. A worship album with the force of an arena show. Guitars and choirs. Choruses that sounded like altars on fire.

And then the release date. September 11, 2001. The same day planes ripped into the Twin Towers. The same morning smoke curled from the Pentagon. The world fractured.

For such a time as this.

Worship was released.[81]

The album became a soundtrack for grief, for prayer, for the aching need to sing when words failed. Whether he knew it or not, Michael W. Smith had just helped pivot CCM into its next chapter—from concerts to congregations, from performance to praise.

The spotlight moved. The gravity shifted back *into* the sanctuary.

Recorded live, the album sounded different. Thousands of voices rising together. Not spectators. Not fans. A congregation. People weren't just listening to Jesus Music anymore—they were singing it. Loud. Corporate. Sacramental.

The record went platinum.[82] CCM's pop ambitions didn't disappear, but its future was clear. The movement that began with hippies strumming choruses on the beaches of California would not end with stadium tours or crossover singles. Its most enduring legacy might be this: congregations lifting their voices together in praise.

But the story didn't stop with Smith. There is a lot more that can and likely *should* be mentioned.

In 2018, Lauren Daigle rose as the new face of crossover success. With her raspy timbre and radio-friendly ballads, *You Say*[83] dominated Billboard charts and earned her two Grammys.[84] For many, Daigle was heir to Amy Grant—bringing faith-inflected lyrics into mainstream pop while still carrying the hopes of evangelical fans.

81. Smith, *Worship*.
82. CBN.com, "Michael W. Smith's Worship Goes Double Platinum," para. 1.
83. Daigle, *You Say*.
84. Schiller, "Lauren Daigle Talks Grammy Wins," paras. 1–2.

And then there was Kirk Franklin. Long before Daigle, Franklin had already disrupted CCM's boundaries. His *Stomp*[85] scandalized some but slipped Black gospel and hip-hop grooves into white evangelical youth groups. Through the 2000s and beyond, Franklin kept breaking molds, reminding CCM that worship was not only guitar-driven and white. His work embodied a larger truth: the Spirit was speaking in multiple tongues, rhythms, and grooves.

By the 2010s, worship music—whether through Chris Tomlin, Hillsong, Bethel, or Elevation—had become the de facto liturgy of evangelicalism. What began in Calvary's coffeehouses now filled stadiums, streamed on Spotify, and scored the devotional life of millions. The irony is clear: what started as Jesus Music, what CCM once sought by mimicking pop, had become the very soundtrack pop itself wanted to mimic. By 2020, mainstream pop stars—Justin Bieber, Selena Gomez, even actors like Chris Pratt—were showing up at Hillsong services, singing the very songs birthed in the church.[86]

Do You Feel It?

Now we circle back. Back to the beginning of our trip.

Time's red letters in 1966—"Is God Dead?"—a question that wasn't just theological, but cultural, semiotic. A sign that the church had lost its microphone. That modernity had turned down the volume on transcendence.

But something else was tuning up.

In deserts and communes, kids in bell-bottoms dosed themselves into visions, chasing the divine through chemistry. In baptismal waves along the Pacific, the Spirit caught them. By 1971, another *Time* cover shouted it clear: *The Jesus Revolution*. From "God is dead" to "Jesus is coming." From silence to song.

Here's the semiotic read: psychedelics cracked open the door, but music blew it off the hinges. LSD lit the spark, but the reverberation—the echo through the decades—was sound.

85. From Kirk Franklin's Nu Nation, *God's Property*.

86. Cho, "All the Celebrities Who've Attended Hillsong," paras. 1–3.

Love Song strummed it soft. Larry Norman screamed it raw. Maranatha! pressed it to vinyl so youth groups could sing it by heart. Amy Grant carried it into the mainstream, platinum and radio-ready. Then came DC Talk, Newsboys, Kirk Franklin, Michael W. Smith, Hillsong, Lauren Daigle. The sound moved from barefoot choruses to billion-dollar stages. From surf breaks to stadium lights. From underground communes to global worship charts.

This chapter hasn't been an exhaustive history. Not even close. It's been a semiotic read—a tracing of signs from Calvary's hippie revival to Contemporary Christian Music to the praise anthems sung today. Not every detail. Not every band. Just the thread. The sign. The sound.

All of which started with psychedelics. LSD.

And so, when you follow it, *if* you follow it, the arc is clear: from LSD to Galilee. From psychedelics to the divine. From "Is God Dead?" to "Jesus Revolution." From the hiss of vinyl to the roar of worship.

Neil Young once laughed when someone asked if rock and roll was the devil's music. He said, "Rock and roll is everybody's fucking music. I think that's where God and the devil shake hands—right there."[87]

That's the crux, isn't it? The sound is bigger than sides. Bigger than boundaries. Bigger than hymnals or hit charts. It carries longing. It carries presence. It carries *us*.

Something is happening here. It always has been.

The sound still reverberates.

Do you feel it? Do you hear it?

And here's the scandal: "it" is never where we expect it. Never where we want it to be. And in this story, "it" arrived through psychedelics. LSD as catalyst. Sound as carrier. Revival as reverberation.

Do you feel it? Do you hear it?

Now . . . let's talk some more about psychedelics.

87. McDonough, *Shakey*, 54.

Part 2: Psychedelics and Semiotics

Chapter 5

"High" Level Overview

"I would never recommend people do this recreationally. But . . . these things have a way of working as a medicine . . ."
—Prince Harry[1]

The setting is a cozy kitchen. Morning sun spills through the window, casting soft gold across the countertops cluttered with the makings of breakfast. The countertop is scattered with supplies—some eggs, maybe bread, a half-emptied carton of orange juice—and there stands a man with a tucked-in button-up shirt, preparing what looks to be an ordinary breakfast.

He picks up an egg and holds it in his hand.

"This," he says, "is your brain."

He turns to the stove where a cast iron skillet sits on an open flame of a gas stove, preheated and waiting. With dramatic precision, he raises the pan and says, "This is drugs."

The camera doesn't flinch. Neither does the man.

Then—crack—the egg drops into the pan, and the sizzle is amplified like it's been turned to eleven on the soundboard of fear. The egg flares out, bubbling, crackling, losing all form.

1. Nelson, "Prince Harry Says He's Used Psychedelics," para. 10.

"This," he says over the sizzle, "is your brain on drugs."

The camera pans in slowly on the egg, now furiously frying in the skillet's heat. Its edges curling and bubbling.

"Any questions?"[2]

* * *

"Just say no to drugs."
—President Ronald Reagan[3]

* * *

If you were a child of the eighties like me, you remember that moment.[4] It wasn't just a TV commercial—it was an imprint. It was the branding of fear. This was the now-infamous 1987 public service announcement campaign "This Is Your Brain On Drugs" sponsored by the Partnership for a Drug-Free America.[5] It didn't just run. It roared. And it ran so often that it embedded itself somewhere deep in our adolescent neurology. That pan. That egg. That line.

And it worked! We believed it. I believed it. I was one of the millions of kids who took it all in like gospel. "Just Say No,"[6] and "I learned it by watching you!"[7] The slogans piled up like Old Testament warnings, each one a holy prohibition framed by the threat of neurological collapse.

I was terrified. Not just of heroin or crack cocaine, but *everything*. Anything remotely associated with the word "drug" sent me into cognitive shutdown. Anything that might fry my brain like an egg in a skillet? No, thank you. Hard pass.

And so, allow me to be very clear—crystal clear—before we go any further: there *are* dangerous drugs out there. Absolutely. Full stop. Our collective

2. Kalamut, "This Is Your Brain . . . ," YouTube video.

3. Reagan, "Address to the Nation on the Campaign Against Drug Abuse."

4. Another is the Cadbury Egg campaign at Eastertime where the kids, dressed up in costume, say at the end of the commercial "Thank you Easter Bunny!" and the other kid mimics a chicken responding, "Bawk Bawk!"

5. Gershon, "Story Behind 'This Is Your Brain,'" para. 1.

6. Reagan, "Just Say No."

7. Bitchute, "I Learned It By Watching You."

work—our human work—is to care for one another, especially our children, and protect each other from that which is destructive. There are chemicals that are addictive, soul-crushing, devastating. That is the purpose of the Controlled Substances Act,[8] or at least it should be. We need systems of education, regulation, and rehabilitation to help us sort the experimental from the medicinal from the recreational, and then to help heal us when the lines are misunderstood. This is wisdom. This is love.

But here's the thing. The word in question—the fulcrum around which all this pivots—is "dangerous."

Because many drugs are.

But not all.

And this, right here, is where the conversation opens—because I want to talk about psychedelics.

And that, it turns out, *may* be an entirely different story.

Psychedelic

* * *

"I feel spiritual when I'm on mushrooms."
—Chelsea Handler[9]

* * *

The word itself still conjures curiosity.

It lands in the ear like incense smoke in the sanctuary—familiar, foreign, and strangely full of promise. *Psychedelic.* A term that didn't even exist a century ago. A term invented to try and say the unsayable. A term built—quite literally—to hold the mystery.

It wasn't coined by a mystic or a high priest of the ancient world. It came from a conversation—mid-century, academic, British. Though the conversation started at the very late part of the nineteenth century,[10] it was back in

8. Ortiz and Preuss, "Controlled Substance Act of 1970."
9. Brown, "Drug Trip That Led Chelsea Handler," para. 1.
10. Partridge, *High Culture*, 4.

the 1950s when two men found themselves pulled together by the strange gravity of a shared curiosity: Aldous Huxley, the novelist and cultural critic who'd already tasted mescaline and lived to write *The Doors of Perception*, and Humphrey Osmond, a psychiatrist on the frontier of hallucinogenic therapy. Together, they were searching for a new word. Something that could hold the weight and wonder of what these compounds were doing to the human mind.

Huxley tried first. In 1953, he proposed the term *phanerothyme*, meaning "to reveal one's soul."[11] And, he offered a rhyme to help it land:

> To make this mundane world sublime, Take half a gram of phanerothyme.[12]

Elegant. Literary. Forgettable.

Osmond countered. After floating a few clunky duds like *psychezymic* (mind fermenting) and *psycherhexic* (mind bursting forth), he offered one that struck gold: *psychedelic*—a word formed from the Greek *psyche* (ψυχή), meaning "mind," and *delein* (δηλείν), meaning "to manifest or make visible."[13] His rhyme?

> To fathom hell or go angelic, Just take a pinch of psychedelic.[14]

That one landed. The word stuck. And with it came a new cultural frame.

More recently, some circles have shifted toward the word *entheogen*, from the Greek *entheos* (ἔνθεος), meaning "the god within."[15] Unlike the clinical tone of psychedelic, this term carries a sacramental feel. These are not merely chemicals, but catalysts for communion—substances said to reveal something beyond, something that can't be fully known, that which is beyond the scientific. As many now claim, these compounds, as the word clearly indicates, reveal, make visible, even manifest, nothing short of love, community, connection, God, and the divine.[16]

Wait—what?

11. Pollan, *How to Change Your Mind*, 163.
12. Stevens, *Storming Heaven*, 57.
13. Weil, *From Chocolate to Morphine*, 93.
14. Stevens, *Storming Heaven*, 57.
15. Partridge, *High Culture*, 4.
16. Pollan, *How to Change Your Mind*, 70–71.

They reveal *God*? They manifest the divine? They make visible one's soul?

So, tell me again how these psychedelics fry my brain like an egg in a hot skillet?

Because here's what wasn't in the after-school specials: while some of these substances are cooked up in sterile labs with pharmaceutical precision, many of them—maybe the most significant ones—have been with us longer than we've been . . . us.

While it is true that in modern times some of these compounds are created in a lab, what we now label as psychedelics have been around for millennia, long before humans became . . . well, humans. Interestingly, there is even a controversial hypothesis known as the stoned ape theory proposed by ethnobotanist and mystic Terence McKenna.[17] The theory states that omnivorous pre-humans would find mind-altering mushrooms and consume them as simple food.

> The theory carefully, somewhat densely, and elegantly suggests that naturally occurring psychedelic compounds—specifically psilocybin—played a decisive role in the emergence of our essential humanness, of the human characteristic of self-reflection.[18]

In other words, the accidental, or at least nonpurposeful, use of psychedelics expanded the minds, brain power, awareness, perception and abilities of our pre-human ancestors and over 100,000 years or more, literally rewired our brains until we became human. This theory blatantly describes psychedelics as one of the important factors, and possibly *the* factor, in the biological evolution that ultimately leads to us, to becoming human.[19]

Since then, in nearly every culture, these plant-based psychedelic medicines have been used for their transcendental properties and for a connection to the spiritual world. Some of the oldest archaeological evidence that people directly interacted with and used psychedelic plants is from about 13,000 years ago![20]

So the idea that this is something new—some Silicon Valley trend or Woodstock-era experiment gone wrong—is simply false. These

17. McKenna, "Stoned Ape Hypothesis."
18. Lin, "Psilocybin, the Mushroom, and Terence McKenna," para. 12.
19. McKenna, *Food of the Gods*, 61–65.
20. Samorini, "Oldest Archeological Data," para. 17.

compounds have been with us. Alongside us. In ritual, in ceremony, in story. Carried by elders and healers, encoded in myth and symbol, swallowed in silence or in song. They are the plants that opened the heavens and the fungi that whispered eternity.

And if that makes you uncomfortable, good. Sit with that discomfort for a moment.

Because maybe we've been asking the wrong question all along.

Maybe the question isn't "How dangerous are these substances?" Maybe the question is "How dangerous is it to forget?" To forget that for thousands of years, across continents and cultures, humans have returned to these plants not for escape—but for revelation. For healing. For memory. For the language that lives beyond words.

Now, to be clear: not all psychedelics are equal. Not all contexts are sacred. Not all usage is wise or life-giving. Intention, preparation, and integration matter deeply. But to dismiss the whole story based on a frying egg commercial is not just uninformed. It's a bit dishonest.

And it's here that we need to shift lenses. If this book is about the question of "where does God show up in the world?" or "is God more often found on the fringe and the 'outside' more than the mainstream and the expected?" then this chapter must begin by naming this: psychedelics, from their very birth into our consciousness, were never *just* drugs.

They were sacraments.

They were portals.

They were ways of knowing and remembering that which can't be captured in doctrine or dogma. They were a means of connection with that which is beyond our everyday horizon. And they are once again rising to the surface in our culture—not as party favors, but as profound questions.

And maybe—just maybe—as answers.

Now that we've cleared the skillet and set aside the propaganda, we can begin. And if we're going to tell the story right, we need to know the key players.

So before we move into the theologies and testimonies, let's start with a brief introduction to the cast of characters—those ancient, earthy, and wildly mysterious plants we've come to call psychedelics.

Because this isn't the story of drugs.

It's the story of revelation.

Mescaline (Peyote)

* * *

"Peyote is a teacher . . . it showed me sound in colors, music in visions."
—Carlos Santana[21]

* * *

Let's begin with the cactus.

Tiny, unassuming, and button-like, *Lophophora williamsii*—more commonly known as peyote[22]—has been quietly growing in the deserts of northern Mexico and the American Southwest for millennia. Not years. Not centuries. *Millennia*. Archaeological evidence suggests that Indigenous communities were using peyote ritually and medicinally at least 5,700 years ago, with remains discovered in the Shumla Caves of Texas dating back to 3700 BCE.[23]

And what makes peyote *peyote*, what turns this little desert plant into a sacrament, is a naturally occurring compound called mescaline.

Mescaline is a psychedelic, but it's not "recreational" in the modern, misunderstood sense. It is a substance that, in ritual and reverence, reveals the divine. Within the Native American Church (NAC), which formally integrates Christian belief with Indigenous spiritual practice, peyote is legally protected for ceremonial use.[24] Its adherents speak of it not as a drug, but

21. Santana et al., *Universal Tone*, 194.
22. Bauer, "Compounds In Psychedelic Cacti," para. 1.
23. El-Seedi et al., "Prehistoric Peyote Use," 238–42.
24. *BBC News Magazine*, "People Who Take Drugs To See God."

as religious sacrament.[25] It is prayer. It is communion. It is a teacher. One that doesn't speak in syllables but in visions, in silence, in that strange space where memory and mystery meet.

To engage peyote is not to escape reality—it's to surrender to it. To face it. To see with spirit eyes what the ordinary eyes have been trained to ignore.

And while mescaline is found in other cacti like *San Pedro* (*Echinopsis pachanoi*) and *Peruvian torch*,[26] it is peyote—small, slow-growing, and sacred—that has carried this medicine through centuries of colonization, criminalization, and cultural erasure.[27] That it still exists today, legally recognized for religious use in the United States, is nothing short of a miracle of resistance.

This is not just chemistry. It's story. It's survival. It's soul.

So yes—while modern science may study mescaline in terms of 5-HT2A receptors and serotonergic pathways,[28] Indigenous wisdom already knew what it was: a bridge. A healer. A gift from the desert floor.

To call it "just a drug" is to miss the point entirely.

* * *

"They [drugs] let you step outside the frame for a while. And when you come back, you can see the picture better."

—George Carlin[29]

* * *

But if peyote carried the soul of the desert, mescaline would eventually find its way into the salons of London and the hills of Hollywood. The cactus crossed the Atlantic—quietly at first—and what it revealed to Indigenous peoples through vision, it whispered to a curious British mystic through prose.

25. Cornell Law School Legal Information Institute, "42 U.S. Code § 1996a."
26. Vamvakopoulou et al., "Mescaline," 109294.
27. Stewart, *Peyote Religion*, 48.
28. Nichols, "Psychedelics," 264–355.
29. Cusick, "George Carlin," para. 15.

If peyote was the sacred cactus of the desert, then Aldous Huxley was its unlikely British prophet.

Born into an aristocratic family of scientists and scholars,[30] Huxley spent much of his life exploring consciousness—not just in fiction, but in philosophy, mysticism, and eventually, psychedelics. By the early 1950s, after surviving war, exile, and near-blindness, Huxley had become increasingly interested in what he called "the antipodes of the mind"—those uncharted inner landscapes only accessible through contemplative practice, meditation, or altered states.[31]

Mescaline gave him the map.

On the morning of May 4, 1953, in the Hollywood Hills, Huxley swallowed a dose of mescaline under the guidance of Dr. Humphry Osmond, a British psychiatrist experimenting with psychedelics as tools for psychotherapy.[32] Huxley's detailed account of the experience became his seminal essay *The Doors of Perception*, a slim book that would go on to influence generations of seekers, artists, and scientists alike.

Huxley wrote of the radical shift in perception he encountered—an unmooring of the self from its filtering system of expectations and language. "The great change was in the realm of objective fact," he wrote, describing how the mind, under mescaline's influence, was no longer organizing the world into categories of use and function. A chair was no longer a chair—it was color, texture, presence. "What had happened to my subjective universe? Gone, gone, gone, dissolved into the glory of things."[33]

For Huxley, this was not hallucination. This was revelation. "Everything shone with the Inner Light and was infinite in its significance," he claimed.[34] It wasn't that mescaline added something unnatural to his vision, it removed the dulling veil of habit and ego that numbs us to wonder.

The experience confirmed what mystics across traditions had long suggested: that perception is spiritual, and that vision—true vision—is a kind of surrender.

30. Watt, *Aldous Huxley*, 366.
31. Huxley, *Heaven & Hell*, 62ff.
32. Jay, "What Happened to Mescaline?," para. 2.
33. Huxley, *Doors of Perception*, 16.
34. Huxley, *Doors of Perception*, 22.

Huxley compared the experience to the beatific vision described by Christian saints.[35] He noted parallels to Meister Eckhart,[36] to the unitive language of the Upanishads,[37] and to the "is-ness" of Zen.[38] This wasn't just exotic metaphor; Huxley was trying to locate the sacramental in the sensory. "The man who comes back through the Door in the Wall," he wrote, "will never be quite the same as the man who went out."[39]

What mescaline revealed to Huxley is what Indigenous practitioners already knew: the sacred is not elsewhere. It is here—hidden in plain sight.

Huxley didn't romanticize the chemical itself. He was careful to insist that psychedelics were "gratuitous graces"[40]—not to be confused with earned spiritual growth or the fruits of disciplined practice. He likened them to a telescope: they extend your vision, yes, but they don't build the muscle required to climb the mountain. Still, he believed they could open the eyes of a culture that had grown spiritually blind. "Most men and women," he wrote, "lead lives at the worst so painful, at the best so monotonous, poor and limited that the urge to escape . . . is and has always been one of the principal appetites of the soul."[41]

Mescaline, he argued, was one doorway—not the only one—but a doorway nonetheless.

* * *

"I think of mescaline as a window. The light is different there."
—Jim Morrison[42]

* * *

And here's the twist that still carries theological weight: Huxley wasn't just interested in the *effects* of mescaline. He was interested in its *implications*. What does it mean, he asked, that a substance—drawn from a cactus—could

35. Huxley, *Doors of Perception*, 73.
36. Huxley, *Doors of Perception*, 42.
37. Huxley, *Heaven & Hell*, 29.
38. Huxley, *Doors of Perception*, 62.
39. Huxley, *Doors of Perception*, 79.
40. Huxley, *Heaven & Hell*, 87.
41. Huxley, *Doors of Perception*, 62.
42. Hopkins and Sugerman, *No One Here Gets Out Alive*, 89.

reveal the same sacred insights described by saints, monks, and mystics across centuries? What does it mean that a molecule from the desert can tear open the curtain between the profane and the holy?

It was a theological question hiding in a chemical compound.

Huxley pushed further. He suggested that "every individual is at once the beneficiary and the victim of the linguistic tradition into which he has been born"[43]—and that psychedelics could short-circuit that tradition just long enough to awaken a deeper perception. They could pull back what he called the "reducing valve" of the brain—a biological filter that normally prevents us from being overwhelmed by the fullness of reality.

To Huxley, mescaline temporarily opens that valve.[44] And what pours through isn't fantasy. It's truth. The kind of truth that echoes across sacraments, Scriptures, and star fields.

So when we say peyote is sacred, we are not saying something new. We are remembering something old. When we say that mescaline reveals, we are not talking about visual effects or ego dissolution. We are talking about that moment when the ground under your feet and the sky above your head start whispering the same thing:

You are in the presence of the holy.

DMT (Ayahuasca)

* * *

> "I did an ayahuasca cleanse . . . it helped me
> let go of things that darkened my past."
> —Lindsay Lohan[45]

* * *

Let's continue, but this time away from the cactus and toward the jungle. With the vine. With the fire. Let's begin with a question passed down not in textbooks, but in smoke and song: What if a plant could speak?

43. Huxley, *Doors of Perception*, 23.
44. Huxley, *Heaven & Hell*, 89.
45. Rvandervest, "Lindsay Lohan Talks About Ayahuasca."

DMT (ayahuasca) is a psychoactive concoction used by Indigenous people of South America for spiritual ceremonies, divination, and healing.[46] Ayahuasca's active ingredient (N,N-Dimethyltryptamine or DMT for short) is derived by boiling two mixtures of plants simultaneously.[47] In the same way as mescaline, it is used as a ritual entheogen and, therefore, as a religious sacrament, as a plant medicine.[48] People from all over the world travel to have ritualized, spiritually enhancing ayahuasca experiences.

But let's not confuse the popularity of the pilgrimage with the origin of the practice. Who used it first? And who still holds the memory?

Ayahuasca has long been central to the cosmologies of Indigenous Amazonian groups such as the Shipibo-Conibo, the Ashaninka, the Kaxinawá, and the Yawanawá, among others—each with its own language, lineage, and liturgical use of the vine.[49] These communities span across what we now call Peru, Brazil, Colombia, and Ecuador, their territories flowing like the rivers themselves—uninterested in the borders drawn on modern maps. For some, the brew is a healer. For others, a prophet. For all, it is not a drug but a teacher. A sacred presence. A co-participant in the world of the spirits. It doesn't just show you things—it communes with you. It doesn't just heal—it remembers.

It is made by combining two distinct plants: the woody *Banisteriopsis caapi* vine and the DMT-containing leaves of *Psychotria viridis*. The vine's β-carbolines inhibit monoamine oxidase enzymes in the gut—enzymes that would otherwise prevent DMT from reaching the brain. It's a biological duet that makes *vision* possible.[50] It's also a sacred recipe passed down not by measurement, but by memory—taught in dreams, shaped by forests.

46. Dobkin de Rios, "Ayahuasca—the Healing Vine," 256–69.
47. Frecska et al., "Therapeutic Potentials of Ayahuasca," para. 1.
48. Pollan, *How to Change Your Mind*, 27.
49. Hay, "Colonization of the Ayahuasca Experience," para. 9.
50. Jiménez-Garrido et al., "Effects of Ayahuasca on Mental Health," para. 1.

* * *

"I have never had a genuine religious experience. I say this with some regret. But the ayahuasca has brought me close to something, something fearful and profound and deadly serious."

—Sting[51]

* * *

Preparation is no small task. The two plants are boiled over a fire for hours, sometimes days. There is no manual. The recipe is received, not written. The fire is tended, the leaves are prayed over, and the brew becomes more than medicine. It becomes an invocation. Rituals are most often held at night and are led by shamans or *ayahuasqueros*,[52] often in silence. *Dietas* are followed. These aren't just temporary food restrictions—they are spiritual fasts. Sacramental disciplines. A kind of embodied preparation that may include abstaining from salt, sugar, meat, sex, or even certain conversations.[53] The goal isn't just purity—it's permission. A way of making space for the medicine to speak. The air thickens. Then begin the *icaros*—those spirit-guided songs that shape not just the ceremony but the inner journey itself.[54] They anchor the space and sometimes steer the vision.[55] These are not embellishments. They are navigational tools for the soul's journey.[56] Often, the room becomes a mirror, reflecting every wound you've tried to bury and every truth you've tried to dodge.

And, what follows is rarely gentle. Effects range from intense visuals and emotional catharsis to purging, revelation, and a dissolving sense of ego. Some see ancestors. Some meet divinity. Many weep. And still others leave having experienced measurable psychological healing—even one dose has been shown to offer significant antidepressant benefit in clinical studies.[57] fMRI studies show modulation in the default mode network, a key neurological circuit tied to self-perception and trauma.[58]

51. Sting, *Broken Music*, 14.
52. Pollan, *How to Change Your Mind*, 27.
53. O'Shaughnessy and Berlowitz, "Amazonian Medicine and the Psychedelic,'" 12.
54. Sherwin et al., "Participant Experiences of Icaros," 149–68.
55. Ruffell et al., "Ayahuasca," 10–11
56. Ruffell et al., "Ayahuasca," 10–11.
57. Jiménez-Garrido et al., "Effects of Ayahuasca," 4075.
58. Ruffell et al., "Ayahuasca," 10–11.

But even as interest grows, so does the risk of extraction without reverence. What happens when the vine is taken but the story is not? When the medicine is imported but the memory is erased?

Ayahuasca is not ours to own. It is ours to honor.

Psilocybin (Magic Mushrooms)

* * *

> "Shrooms are full of shit. That is the whole story. Grown in shit, it's their essence: they try to humble you in these ways that bring you down to their level."
>
> —A. D. Aliwat[59]

* * *

From cactus to vine, we've followed these ancient medicines across geography and lineage. We've walked through desert prayers and jungle chants. We've sat with the sacred bitterness of peyote and the smoky, slow-brewed visions of ayahuasca. Each one rooted in community. In reverence. In songs older than Scripture. But now, the path turns downward.

Because the next sacrament doesn't rise up toward the sun. It doesn't need a tree or a vine or a woven vine string of tradition to announce its presence.

It grows underground.

It doesn't bloom. It waits.

It doesn't reach. It reveals.

From the dry floor of the Sonoran Desert to the dense, pulsing canopy of the Amazon, we now descend to the forest floor—into the quiet, holy rot where psilocybin begins. Hidden. Humble. And utterly alive.

This one doesn't shout. It doesn't dazzle with flame or fragrance. It speaks through decay and emergence. It waits to be found by those willing to look low enough.

Because the mushroom doesn't grow tall.

59. Aliwat, *In Limbo*, 480.

It grows true.

Psilocybin, commonly known as "magic mushrooms," is produced by hundreds of species of fungi. But its real magic may be what it produces in us. Of all the classic psychedelics, psilocybin has perhaps attracted the most modern scientific attention. Not just for its ability to generate vivid, mystical encounters—but for the healing those encounters seem to bring. From anxiety and addiction to depression and despair, studies continue to show what Indigenous people have known for generations: these mushrooms don't just open your mind. They mend it.[60]

And their history goes back further than most are willing to admit, at least 9,000 years.[61]

Some of the oldest human images ever carved depict mushrooms. Cave walls in North Africa. Rock art in Spain. Archaeological sites across Mesoamerica.[62] The word that Bernardino de Sahagún gave to these mushrooms is *teonanácatl*, a Nahuatl word that has been translated into English as "sacred mushroom" or "flesh of the gods," which was consumed as a sacrament during Aztec religious rituals.[63] The statue of Xochipilli, the Aztec god of flowers, sits covered in carvings that R. Gordon Wasson believed to be psychedelic mushrooms, each etched like a whisper of memory into stone.[64]

These were not simple mushrooms. Not just something to eat. They were sacred to these people.[65] They were cosmological.

Wasson is certainly included in the long list of notable names connected to the rise of psychedelics, specifically psilocybin. It was Wasson's ability to proliferate the mythos—to make the world believe that magic mushrooms were, well, magic—that changed everything. He helped awaken a public imagination that had long forgotten that mushrooms could be mystical.

60. See Grob, "Psychiatric Research with Hallucinogens"; Nichols, "Psychedelics"; and George et al., "Ancient Roots."

61. Akers et al., "Prehistoric Mural in Spain."

62. Akers et al., "Prehistoric Mural in Spain."

63. Singer, "Mycological Investigations on TEONANÁCATL."

64. Wasson, "Role of 'Flowers.'"

65. Winkelman, "Introduction: Evidence for Entheogen."

By day, Wasson was a Wall Street man. In 1941, he was named vice president for public relations at J. P. Morgan.[66] But he had a second life. A quieter one. A slower one. One that knelt low to the earth and searched under leaves. He studied mushrooms.

* * *

> "There are aspects of [mushrooms] that the places you can go in your brain are much deeper and more healing than anything else."
> —Kristin Bell[67]

* * *

That journey began in 1927, on his honeymoon in the Catskill Mountains. His wife, Valentina Pavlova Guercken—a Russian pediatrician—had come across a patch of wild mushrooms. She recognized them. Picked them. Ate them. Wasson refused. He was afraid. But she lived. More than that, she thrived. The conversation that followed sparked something that wouldn't go out.[68] Together, they began exploring the world of mushrooms, and their curiosity eventually led them far beyond the Catskills—to the Sierra Mazateca of southern Mexico, in search of something far older than folklore.[69] They wanted to witness the Mazatec Mushroom Ritual, a sacred ceremony rooted in thousands of years of practice.[70] And it was on this trip that they met María Sabina, a *curandera*, a traditional healer who carried within her the memory and the music of the mushrooms.[71] She never described psilocybin in scientific terms. She called them "*niños santos*"—holy children.[72] She was the keeper of a language spoken not in words, but in visions. In stillness. In soundless encounter.

But the ritual is not for tourists. It is not for cultural outsiders. It is sacred and traditionally used to locate something lost—a missing object, a sick soul, a broken body. Wasson, not needing anything found, invented a story.

66. Pfister, "R. Gordon Wasson—1898–1986."
67. Guerrasio, "Kristen Bell Says She Did Hallucinogenic Mushrooms," para. 4.
68. Pfister, "R. Gordon Wasson—1898–1986," 12.
69. Wasson, "Drugs," para. 1–9.
70. Wasson, "Drugs," para. 1–9.
71. Guzmán, "Hallucinogenic Mushrooms in Mexico."
72. Pollan et al., "Tragic Story of Maria."

He told María he was concerned for the whereabouts of his son back home. With this fabrication, the door opened. María invited him in.[73]

She led him through the ritual. And more—she allowed him to take her photograph, on the condition that it remain private. But Wasson did not honor her request. He published her picture. Her name. The name of her village. The ritual that had been protected for centuries—protected from empire, from outsiders, from exploitation—was now broadcast across the globe.[74]

In 1957, Wasson and Valentina published a two-volume work titled *Mushrooms, Russia and History*. But it was the *Life* magazine article, "Seeking the Magic Mushroom," that launched a cultural moment.[75] It reached millions. It introduced the idea of psilocybin to the Western imagination. And suddenly, the veil was torn.

Wasson became famous. He gave lectures. Received invitations. His name was etched into the psychedelic canon.

María, however, died in poverty.[76]

She was said to be the first *curandera* to allow a Westerner to participate in the ancient mushroom ceremony. And once the story was out, the seekers came. In droves. Hundreds, maybe thousands. It's rumored that Bob Dylan, John Lennon, and Keith Richards found their way to her door.[77] Along with backpackers, journalists, scholars, and self-proclaimed spiritual pilgrims. They came to find something. But they took more than they knew.

Her community, once her sanctuary, turned against her. Her home was burned. Her son was murdered. She was jailed. She was ostracized.[78] The ritual remained—but the reverence was gone. What had been hidden in sacred trust was now consumed by Western hunger.

The story that followed—the one that repeats again and again across continents and cultures—is one of extraction. Wasson didn't discover anything. He revealed what had been intentionally kept hidden. And the language of

73. Pollan, *How to Change Your Mind,* 114.
74. Wasson, "Drugs."
75. Wasson, "Seeking the Magic Mushroom."
76. Gregoire, "Inside the Movement to Decolonize Psychedelic Pharma."
77. Feinberg, *Devil's Book of Culture History*, 151–53.
78. Gregoire, "Inside the Movement to Decolonize Psychedelic Pharma."

"discovery" he used—the colonial echo of a world that thinks knowledge only begins when the West arrives—must be named and repented.

Because that story, too, is part of the psychedelic revival. And that story, too, must be told.

Their account of the trip to Mexico was featured on the cover of *Life*, reaching over twelve million readers.[79] It was this very article that sparked Timothy Leary's own journey, launching a chain reaction of experimentation that would define a generation.

But before we get to Leary, there's one more detail.

One more footnote in this parable of revelation and ruin.

The trip to Mexico—the trip that brought Wasson to María, and María to the world . . . it was fully funded by the CIA through a program known as MK-Ultra.[80]

And yet . . . the mushroom remains.

* * *

> "Everyone thought I was crazy. I bit this guy's ear off . . . I did all this stuff, and once I got introduced to 'shrooms . . . my whole life changed. To think where I was—almost suicidal—to this now . . . It's amazing medicine."
>
> —Mike Tyson[81]

* * *

Psilocybin, once ingested, slows the noise. It softens the walls between self and world. Modern brain scans show it quiets the part of the brain responsible for our internal monologue—what some call the ego, others call the critic, and still others call the liar. In its place, something else rises: spaciousness, connection, mystery. People report encountering divine presence, long-forgotten memories, or messages of forgiveness that have eluded them for decades.[82]

79. Burleigh, "Psychedelic Trip to Timothy Leary's Catalina Resort in Mexico," cover.
80. See Tylš et al., "Psilocybin." More on the CIA's role in chapter 6.
81. Reuters, "Mike Tyson Says Psychedelics Saved His Life," paras. 6–10.
82. Tylš et al., "Psilocybin," 347–48.

In clinical studies, this tiny fungal gift has been shown to relieve depression, anxiety, addiction, and even terminal fear. Not because it numbs the pain. But because it rearranges it. Like a holy therapist who doesn't speak, but listens with your own mind.[83]

But if we receive this sacrament without remembering its story, we are no better than the ones who came to María, took what they wanted, and left nothing but ashes.

Psilocybin is not a hack. It is not a shortcut. It is not a Western breakthrough.

It is a sacred encounter that begins in the dirt and ends in the sky.

It speaks through Indigenous mouths, not lab coats. It sings in *icaros*, not TED Talks. And its truth—its power—was not born in Petri dishes, but in whispered prayers over flickering candles in Mazatec homes.

To eat the mushroom is to listen. To remember. To acknowledge what was stolen.

Because María wasn't just a healer. She was a prophet. A psalmist. A theologian with dirt on her hands and stars in her mouth. And what she offered wasn't just a plant. It was a way of being.

Western medicine may describe psilocybin as a serotonin agonist or a neural reset. But María—really the culture in which she was formed—knew better.

She wasn't just holding mushrooms. She was holding mystery. She was holding the "flesh of the gods," as they called it. And somehow, that phrase lingers—like incense—long after the ceremony ends. Because once you hear it, it's hard not to see the echoes. A sacred meal. A broken body. A presence that invites transformation. Psilocybin, like Communion, is not a thing to be used—it's a presence to be received. A sacrament that doesn't just alter consciousness but re-members what was fractured. It stitches story to soul. Earth to spirit. Us to each other.

This isn't about ideas. This is about encounter. What María presided over wasn't a lecture—it was a liturgy. A ritual way of knowing that begins in the body and radiates outward like ripples.

83. Tylš et al., "Psilocybin," 347.

And if it reveals what's hidden, then it may also reveal something about the church itself. About what we've remembered. And what we've buried.

Because maybe the mushroom doesn't just offer visions. Maybe it offers return.

And suddenly . . . the egg is back. The hot pan. The sizzle. That old commercial told us that drugs fry the mind. That they destroy. That they devour.

But what if—not *all* of them do?

What if some reveal? What if some restore?

What if some don't fry the brain . . . but feed the soul?

What if the true scandal wasn't the mushroom . . . but that *flesh of the gods* could be received at all?

And what if the table was never the problem? What if it's been the invitation all along?

But before we break that bread, before we enter the sanctuary . . . Let's talk about LSD.

Chapter 6

And Then . . . There Was LSD

"I lay down and sank into not an unpleasant intoxicated-like condition, characterized by an extremely stimulated imagination . . ."
—Albert Hofmann, journal entry April 16, 1943[1]

It comes from another fungus—ergot—a dark, unassuming growth that appears on the heads of rye and wheat.[2] It's an unlikely portal to the infinite, hiding in the ordinary bread of the world. If peyote was the teacher from the desert, ayahuasca the prophet from the jungle, and psilocybin the priest of the forest floor, then LSD is the trickster-chemist—born not in ceremony but in the white coat of a Basel laboratory, in mid-century Europe. It emerged from the marriage of ancient grain and modern science, a reminder that the sacred sometimes slips in through side doors we didn't even know were open.

Like the other sacraments, LSD has mind-freeing capabilities. But it also carries a strange dual citizenship—rooted in the natural world and yet wholly birthed in human hands. It is both an origin story and a cautionary tale, an invitation to climb the ladder of the mind toward visions that may or may not be ours to keep. And that word—*cautionary*—deserves a moment. Every tradition that carried these medicines also built a container

1. Hofmann, *LSD, My Problem Child*, 47.
2. Hofmann, *LSD, My Problem Child*, 38–39.

around them, or a safety net, if you will: a guide, a ritual, a community of elders who knew what they were doing and protected each other through the journey. Strip the container, clear the safety net, and keep only the substance, and the results can be devastating. Not theoretical. Real. The history of psychedelics is a history of both revelation and rupture. And yet, the stories keep coming . . .

In the documentary *Have A Good Trip: Adventures in Psychedelics*,[3] actors, comedians, and musicians speak about their encounters with this particular sacrament—part testimony, part parable. Their stories ripple with the same refrain: LSD opens something. Sometimes it's beauty. Sometimes it's terror. Sometimes it's both at once, inseparable. And maybe that's the point—because revelation has never promised to be safe.

* * *

"I took acid and said 'Oh . . . I see. That makes sense.'"
—Carrie Fisher[4]

* * *

Bicycle Day

Just so you know . . . the reality is that it wasn't really an accident. Not really.

The actual discovery was, in many ways, planned and predictable. Some argue that the true story of LSD began in 1936, when two researchers isolated the structure of lysergic acid at the Rockefeller Institute for Medical Research.[5] But the truth is, very few people really know—or care—about that. The man who became the symbolic father of LSD—and later called it his "problem child"[6]—was Albert Hofmann.

Hofmann had just completed his graduate studies in chemistry at the University of Zurich in 1929 when he joined the Sandoz Company as a pharmaceutical-chemical researcher. His doctoral work had already shown his fascination with the building blocks of nature. "Making use of the

3. Donick, dir., *Have A Good Trip*.
4. Donick, dir., *Have A Good Trip*.
5. Partridge, *High Culture*, 195.
6. Hofmann, *LSD, My Problem Child*, 23.

gastrointestinal juice of the vineyard snail," he later wrote, he "accomplished the enzymatic degradation of chitin, the structural material of which the shells, wings, and claws of insects, crustaceans, and other lower animals are composed."[7] He earned his doctorate with distinction, and was promptly tasked at Sandoz with studying plants.

The menu of possible research paths read like a strange botanical tarot: foxglove (*Digitalis*), Mediterranean squill (*Scilla maritima*), and ergot of rye (*Claviceps purpurea* or *Secale cornutum*). Searching for a compound to induce childbirth, Hofmann chose ergot of rye—a fateful choice that, in many ways, began the world's LSD journey.[8] As we move forward, do not forget this unassuming fungus! Ergot—older than the temples, a shadowy companion in humanity's search for the divine, whispered of in ancient rites—now steps once again onto history's stage, the origin of the modern discovery of LSD, and perhaps, a hidden voice in the earliest days of the Christian church.[9]

Centuries passed. The temples fell. And now—Switzerland, 1938.

After years of ergot research, Hofmann produced the twenty-fifth compound of lysergic acid derivatives, hence LSD-25.[10] This is why the creation of LSD wasn't really an accident: it was the fruit of methodical research. At the time, the new substance seemed unremarkable. The lab tested it on rats, who appeared merely "energetic." But how would a rat describe visions? How would a rat tell you that time had become liquid, or that a chair was no longer a chair? For five years, LSD-25 was shelved and forgotten.[11]

Then, for reasons even he couldn't fully explain, Hofmann decided to revisit the compound in 1943. During the re-synthesis of LSD-25, he accidentally ingested a trace amount. The lab notebook records what followed:

> Last Friday, April 16, 1943, I was forced to interrupt my work in the laboratory in the middle of the afternoon to proceed home being affected by a remarkable restlessness, combined with a slight dizziness. At home I lay down and sank into a not unpleasant intoxicated-like condition, characterized by an extremely

7. Hofmann, *LSD, My Problem Child*, 36.
8. Hofmann, *LSD, My Problem Child*, 37.
9. More on that in chapter 7.
10. Hofmann, *LSD, My Problem Child*, 44.
11. Pollan, *How to Change Your Mind*, 29.

> stimulated imagination. In a dreamlike state, with eyes closed (I found the daylight to be unpleasantly glaring), I perceived an uninterrupted stream of fantastic pictures, extraordinary shapes with intense, kaleidoscopic play of colors. After some two hours this condition faded away.[12]

A rat could never tell you that. And in the symbolic economy of discovery, such an experience needed confirmation. Hofmann resolved to conduct a test and record what he experienced.

Three days later—April 19, 1943, at precisely 4:20 PM—he embarked on the first intentional experimental dosing of LSD-25. He ingested what we now know was a massive amount and began to record the onset:[13] "Beginning dizziness, feeling anxiety, visual distortions, symptoms of paralysis, desire to laugh."[14]

Even finishing these notes took "great effort."[15] Deciding he would be safer at home, Hofmann asked his assistant to accompany him there. Due to wartime restrictions on cars, he mounted his bicycle.[16] Jay Stevens describes that ride:

> [He] pedaled off into a suddenly anarchic universe. In Hofmann's mind this wasn't the familiar boulevard that led home, but a street painted by Salvador Dalí, a funhouse roller coaster where the buildings yawned and rippled . . . Whatever mechanism that translated thoughts into speech . . . was broken. When [Hofmann's assistant] reached Hofmann's house, he found his patient to be physically sound, but mentally . . . hovering near the ceiling.[17]

Hofmann was high. *Really* high.

On that ride home, "everything in my field of vision wavered and was distorted as if seen in a curved mirror." Once inside, his "surroundings had transformed themselves in more terrifying ways."[18] Oddly, he craved milk and drank two liters over the evening. The neighbor who brought it was

12. Hofmann, *LSD, My Problem Child*, 47.
13. Stevens, *Storming Heaven*, 4.
14. Hofmann, *LSD, My Problem Child*, 48.
15. Hofmann, *LSD, My Problem Child*, 48.
16. Gibson, "This Bicycle Day, Celebrate," para. 1.
17. Stevens, *Storming Heaven*, 5.
18. Hofmann, *LSD, My Problem Child*, 48.

not, to his perception, a kindly Samaritan but a "malevolent, insidious witch with a colored mask."[19] The semiotics here are vivid: milk—a primal symbol of nurture—reframed as threat, the maternal turned monstrous.

By morning, the terror had passed.

> A sensation of well-being and renewed life flowed through me. Breakfast tasted delicious and gave me extraordinary pleasure. When I later walked out into the garden, in which the sun shone now after a spring rain, everything glistened and sparkled in a fresh light. The world was as if newly created. All my senses vibrated in a condition of highest sensitivity, which persisted for the entire day.[20]

Here is the hinge of the LSD story: the night before, a witch's mask; the morning after, Eden restored.

Thus ended the first *intentional* LSD trip—a journey that would become an origin myth for the psychedelic age. In 1985, a Northern Illinois University professor hosted a celebration of this day at his home, dubbing it "Bicycle Day," a name now sacred in the psychedelic calendar.[21]

It's worth noting that LSD was first synthesized on November 16, 1938. Just one month later, on December 19, 1938, humanity split the atom.[22] In one of Hofmann's final interviews before his death in 2008, he was asked about this strange pairing—the birth of the atomic bomb and the birth of what he called "the bomb for consciousness." His reply was characteristically understated:

> I don't know if it was a coincidence or probably no coincidence exists in this world. In any case it is strange. It is true that the ordinary bomb is to the atomic bomb what an ordinary intoxicant is to LSD.[23]

Two bombs. One to vaporize matter. One to dissolve the boundaries of the mind.

19. Hofmann, *LSD, My Problem Child*, 48.
20. Hofmann, *LSD, My Problem Child*, 50–51.
21. McMillan, "Bicycle Day."
22. US Department of Energy, "Manhattan Project," para. 2.
23. Walker, dir., *How To Change Your Mind*.

Experimentation

* * *

"I woke up and I told the friend I was with that I know what the answer to life is. It's to love each other."

—A$AP ROCKY[24]

* * *

Not long after Hofmann's legendary bicycle ride, Sandoz Laboratories stepped onto the world stage with their strange new chemical. They gave LSD a brand name—Delysid[25]—and began promoting it as a potential cure for everything from schizophrenia to alcoholism, criminal behavior to sexual "perversions."[26] Just as acetaminophen becomes Tylenol in the pharmacy, Delysid was simply LSD in a lab coat.

Their rollout method? What we might now call *crowdsourced science.* Sandoz Laboratory knew this compound could do something profound—possibly amazing, possibly terrifying—to the human mind. But beyond that? They were flying blind. So, they extended an open invitation to researchers of almost any stripe: try Delysid, take notes, and send us your results. And "researcher" was defined loosely. If you had credentials—or if you could simply convince someone at Sandoz you were conducting *some* form of inquiry—they would ship you a generous supply of Delysid at no charge, with the polite expectation that you would share your observations. This practice, astonishing as it sounds today, ran from 1949 until 1966 with remarkably few changes.[27]

Long before my own 1970s and 1980s upbringing—when drug education was distilled into frying-pan metaphors and "this is your brain on drugs" PSAs—LSD had worn a very different face. As we've already seen, its early reputation wasn't one of danger or countercultural rebellion, but of possibility. In those first years, it carried the glow of scientific promise—bright enough to attract some of the most respected minds in medicine and psychology.

24. Donick, dir., *Have A Good Trip.*
25. Pollan, *How to Change Your Mind*, 142.
26. DEA Public Affairs, "LSD," paras. 4–5.
27. Pollan, *How to Change Your Mind*, 143.

One of those minds, whom we've already met in our earlier naming of psychedelics, was Dr. Humphry Osmond, the British-born psychiatrist who, through his conversations with Aldous Huxley, coined the very word *psychedelic*—"mind-manifesting." Even the term itself is semiotic: a sign pointing not to the substance, but to its effect—the bringing forth of what is hidden. Osmond had grown up and studied in England, but it was during his career in Canada, at the Weyburn Mental Hospital in Saskatchewan, that he began his pioneering work. He believed schizophrenia stemmed from a chemical imbalance in the brain and saw psychedelics as a way to "enter the world" of his patients—not through empathy alone, but through direct symbolic experience.[28] What began as a study in pathology soon became a search for transcendence. Osmond became fascinated by the conditions that made mystical experience more likely—the interplay of set and setting, the symbolic architecture of the room, the ritual of preparation.

It was here that Al Hubbard entered the frame. He was an enigmatic pioneer in psychedelic history—equal parts mystic, entrepreneur, and provocateur, and once a rumrunner turned OSS covert operative, reputed to have smuggled arms during World War II in exchange for a presidential pardon.[29] Nicknamed the "Johnny Appleseed of LSD,"[30] he introduced the drug to over 6,000 individuals: scientists, clergy, politicians, and cultural luminaries alike.[31] He carried an almost evangelistic conviction that LSD, given in the right context, could catalyze profound transformation. Hubbard became Osmond's guide in this territory, teaching him that the container matters as much as the content. The trip wasn't just chemistry—it was liturgy. Osmond adopted many of Hubbard's methods, making his research sessions less like sterile laboratory trials and more like carefully crafted rites of passage within a sanctuary space.[32]

Osmond's credibility was such that he convinced British politician Christopher Mayhew to undertake a guided mescaline session—televised live by the BBC.[33] It was, in its own way, a national sacrament: a public figure stepping

28. Costandi, "Looking Back," para. 2
29. Holden, "Hubbard, Al (1901–1982)," paras. 1, 21.
30. Holden, "Hubbard, Al (1901–1982)," para. 1.
31. Fahey, "Original Captain Trips."
32. Costandi, "Looking Back."
33. "Panorama," 13.

into a mystery before the eyes of the nation. In that moment, psychedelics weren't framed as dangerous—they were framed as worthy of witness.

His work with LSD and alcoholism was equally groundbreaking. The numbers were startling—about a 50 percent success rate in helping chronic alcoholics achieve long-term sobriety after LSD-assisted therapy.[34] This research drew the attention of Bill Wilson, co-founder of Alcoholics Anonymous. Wilson's own recovery had been ignited by a sudden, spontaneous spiritual awakening in 1934—a blinding moment of grace he credited entirely to God. When he later encountered LSD, he recognized something familiar in it. Could this be a similar door? Could chemistry do what grace had done for him—strip the ego bare and let God in? He said that it helped him eliminate the barriers that stood in the way of one's direct experience with God.[35] His first journey was taken with Aldous Huxley and Dr. Betty Eisner, one of his therapists at the time. Eisner was an accomplished scientist in her own right, and like Osmond, she saw psychedelics not as recreational diversions but as catalysts for transformation.[36]

Wilson later wrote in "*Pass It On*":

> It is a generally acknowledged fact in spiritual development that ego reduction makes the influx of God's grace possible. If, therefore, under LSD we can have a temporary reduction, so that we can better see what we are and where, and where we are going, well, that might be of some help. The goal might become clearer. So I consider LSD to be of some value to some people, and practically no damage to anyone.[37]

Here is the language of mystics disguised in the mouth of a pragmatist. Ego reduction. Grace. Clarity of goal. This was not about chemical escape—it was about thinning the veil between the self and the Source. In a 1957 letter, Wilson reflected:

> I am certain that the LSD experiment has helped me very much. I find myself with a heightened color perception and an appreciation of beauty almost destroyed by my years of depression.[38]

34. Bleyer, "Radical New Approach to Beating Addiction," para. 16.
35. Alcoholics Anonymous, "*Pass It On*," 370–71.
36. Hartigan, *Bill W.*, 177–79.
37. Alcoholics Anonymous, "*Pass It On*," 371–72.
38. Macbride, "'I Am Certain,'" para. 5.

For Wilson, and for Osmond, the work was never just pharmacology. It was about building a bridge—a symbolic and chemical bridge—between brokenness and beauty, between addiction and awakening. LSD was not the destination; it was a signpost pointing toward the holy.

The optimism was palpable. From the labs of Sandoz to the pages of *Time*, LSD seemed destined to be medicine for the mind, perhaps even a sacrament for the soul. But as the 1960s progressed, this bright narrative began to bend. Not everyone who took notice of LSD was chasing enlightenment or healing. In the shadows, another set of "researchers" had been watching closely—ones whose goals had little to do with grace, and everything to do with control.

MK-Ultra

* * *

> "In the 1950's and early 1960's, the agency gave mind-altering drugs to hundreds of unsuspecting Americans . . . Many of the human guinea pigs were mental patients, prisoners, drug addicts, and prostitutes—people who could not fight back."
>
> —*The New York Times*[39]

* * *

In December of 1974, *The New York Times* ran a story that hit like a thunderclap: the Central Intelligence Agency—chartered to operate outside US borders—had been conducting illegal domestic operations, including experiments on its own citizens.[40] It cracked open a door the government had worked hard to keep sealed for decades. Under mounting pressure, President Gerald Ford ordered an inquiry, appointing Vice President Nelson Rockefeller to lead what became known as the Rockefeller Commission. Its mandate reached beyond the CIA to other federal agencies, but it was here—through a sliver of public sunlight—that the world first glimpsed the outlines of MK-Ultra.[41]

39. Weiner, "Sidney Gottlieb, 80, Dies," para. 3.
40. Gross, "CIA's Secret Quest," para. 3.
41. CIA, Project MK-ULTRA.

The problem? By then, much of the paper trail had already been burned—literally. A year earlier, at the direction of CIA leadership, swaths of files had been destroyed. What remained was heavily redacted, like Scripture with the most damning verses blotted out. Even so, one title of one program slipped through: MK-Ultra.[42]

More committees, commissions, and task forces followed, but MK-Ultra remained the shadow in the room—an outline without a clear face. The fragments that survived told a story stranger and darker than anyone had imagined.

MK-Ultra was a clandestine CIA program, launched in 1953, dedicated to testing the boundaries of the human mind. Its aim? To find chemical, psychological, and even spiritual levers that, if pulled, could control behavior—especially in interrogation. "Truth drugs." Mind control. Behavior modification.[43] This wasn't just science; it was sorcery with a government grant.

When the Freedom of Information Act cracked open a few more files in 1976—thanks largely to author and researcher John D. Marks—one bizarre fact jumped out: the CIA had tried to buy 100 million doses of LSD from Sandoz Laboratories (yes . . . that Sandoz, the one that branded LSD as Delysid and employed Hofmann, who first synthesized it).[44] They were convinced, at least for a time, that lysergic acid could be weaponized. The agency admitted to administering at least 25,000 doses to human subjects between the late 1940s and early 1960s, only to conclude—after years of covert trials—that LSD's effects were too unpredictable to be reliable for interrogations.[45] But the unpredictability that frustrated the CIA? That was exactly what cracked the culture wide open.

And behind those statistics were real people—often unsuspecting—whose lives became the proving ground for the agency's experiments. Some subjects were dosed without their consent—prisoners, hospital patients, even casual acquaintances of agency front men. Others volunteered, signing up

42. CIA, Project MK-ULTRA.

43. Select Committee to Study Governmental Operations, *Final Report*, 390ff.

44. *New York Times*, "C.I.A. Considered Big LSD Purchase," para. 1.

45. Gross, "CIA's Secret Quest," para. 1.

for research without realizing the CIA was behind it. The official line was "scientific exploration." The hidden line was "weapons testing."[46]

One of those volunteers was Ken Kesey, a young writer working nights at the Menlo Park Veterans Hospital (which in part inspired his novel *One Flew Over The Cuckoo's Nest*). For $75, Kesey swallowed his first government-approved dose of LSD. Michael Pollan, looking back, quipped, "With Ken Kesey, the CIA had turned on exactly the wrong man."[47]

Kesey didn't just take the trip—he took the map. Calling it "the revolt of the guinea pigs,"[48] he gathered a loose tribe of artists, dropouts, and dreamers who became the Merry Pranksters.[49] Their mission wasn't covert; it was carnival.

Carolyn "Mountain Girl" Adams, one of the Pranksters—and later Kesey's lover—remembered the gatherings they called Acid Tests.[50] "We were creating a safe place for people to get high,"[51] she said. The "safe place" often took the form of a garbage can or picnic cooler filled with LSD-laced Kool-Aid, ladled out like communion wine at a revival meeting.[52] No one checked IDs. If you were there, you were "in the know." And if you weren't . . . well, you might find yourself baptized into a new consciousness about forty-five minutes after your first sip.[53]

From the Bay Area outward, the Pranksters toured the country in a bus named *Further*, painted in riotous color like a moving icon of the psychedelic gospel.[54] They weren't just throwing parties; they were initiating America into a new liturgy—one in which music, light, and altered states blurred the lines between audience and priest, sanctuary and street. They had three goals: to evangelize LSD use, to promote Kesey's novel *Sometimes a Great Notion*, and to make pilgrimage to an upstate New York commune whispered about in psychedelic circles—a place where two

46. Weiner, "Sidney Gottlieb, 80, Dies."
47. Pollan, *How to Change Your Mind*, 206.
48. Pollan, *How to Change Your Mind*, 206.
49. Pollan, *How to Change Your Mind*, 206.
50. Wolfe, *Electric Kool-Aid Acid Test*, 266ff.
51. Weller, "LSD, Ecstasy, and a Blast," para. 15.
52. Weller, "LSD, Ecstasy, and a Blast," para. 15.
53. Profit, dir., *American Dope*.
54. Wolfe, *Electric Kool-Aid Acid Test*, 67–69.

former Harvard psychologists were said to be mapping the boundaries of the mind like cartographers of an unseen world.[55]

* * *

"... spiritual ecstasy, religious revelation, and union
with God were now directly accessible ..."
—Timothy Leary[56]

* * *

Pollan writes, "a case can be made that the cultural upheaval we call the 1960's began with a CIA mind-control experiment gone awry."[57] And really—when you unleash a busload of psychedelic evangelists across a country already simmering with civil rights protests, anti-war marches, and a growing counterculture, what else could happen?

The acid the Pranksters used—and, honestly, most of the LSD circulating on the West Coast between 1965 and 1967—came from one man: Augustus Owsley Stanley III, known simply as "Owsley" or "the Bear."[58] As we noted when we met him in an earlier chapter, he was an audio engineer for the Grateful Dead and an underground chemist.[59] Owsley became legendary for the purity of his "Owsley Acid."[60] His product fueled the *Magical Mystery Tour*, Three Dog Night, the Dead, and countless unnamed seekers.[61]

Owsley's ambition was nothing less than global transformation—turning on the entire world. To scale up, he took on an apprentice: Tim Scully. Yes, *that* Tim Scully—the same mind we met back in chapter 2 when we traced the Brotherhood of Eternal Love and their fabled Orange Sunshine. Scully first crossed paths with Owsley at the Watts Acid Test in February 1966,[62] and the connection would eventually lead him, alongside partner Nick Sand, to produce the very Orange Sunshine that became the Brotherhood's sacrament of choice. The pieces were beginning to connect.

55. Charters, *Beats*, 306–16.
56. Minutaglio and Davis, *Most Dangerous Man in America*, 1.
57. Pollan, *How to Change Your Mind*, 207.
58. Ulrich, *Timothy Leary Project*, 26.
59. Pareles, "Jerry Garcia of Grateful Dead."
60. Brown, "'Bear' Stanley, Who Made LSD."
61. Freeman, "Dark, One-Dog Night."
62. Minutaglio and Davis, *Most Dangerous Man in America*, 1.

* * *

"The first couple times I tripped, I really did believe that the world would be a better place if every single person . . . the planet would be a better place if everybody took acid once."

—David Cross[63]

* * *

Meanwhile, the White House was looking for an enemy it could name. President Nixon—ever attuned to the optics of power—was under fire for being soft on the counterculture. In July 1971, in a now-infamous recorded meeting, Nixon and his advisors discussed finding "some bad guy" to personify the War on Drugs. Treasury Secretary John Connally urged him to choose one name. Someone in the room said, "Leary." Nixon didn't miss a beat: "Well, we've got room in the prisons for him."[64] Not long after, Nixon would publicly dub Timothy Leary "the most dangerous man in America."[65]

The phrase was more than political theater. Years later, former Nixon domestic policy chief John Ehrlichman admitted in a 1994 interview that the War on Drugs was never about drugs—it was a deliberate political weapon. "The Nixon campaign in 1968, and the Nixon White House after that, had two enemies: the antiwar left and Black people," Ehrlichman stated. "We knew we couldn't make it illegal to be either against the war or Black [people], but by getting the public to associate the hippies with marijuana and Blacks with heroin, and then criminalizing both heavily, we could disrupt those communities. We could arrest their leaders, raid their homes, break up their meetings, and vilify them night after night on the evening news . . . Did we know we were lying about the drugs? Of course we did."[66]

In that calculus, psychedelics—especially LSD—became visual shorthand for the long-haired, anti-establishment youth Nixon wanted to neutralize. And Timothy Leary, with his unabashed call to "turn on, tune in, drop out,"[67] was the perfect lightning rod.

63. Donick, dir., *Have A Good Trip*.
64. Minutaglio and Davis, *Most Dangerous Man in America*, 1.
65. Shapiro, "Nixon's Manhunt for the High Priest," para. 2.
66. Baum, "Legalize It All," para. 2
67. Starbacker, "Tune In, Turn On, Step Up."

One year after that meeting in the White House, federal agents mounted a sweeping raid—Operation BEL—on August 5, 1972, targeting the Brotherhood of Eternal Love across California, Oregon, and Hawaii. In what authorities called the largest drug bust in US history, over 450 law enforcement officers executed twenty-nine search warrants, arresting more than forty members and associates, and seizing massive quantities of contraband: more than 1.5 tons of hashish, 3,500 LSD tablets, weapons, and cash.[68] The operation struck at every layer of the Brotherhood's network—from their Laguna Beach storefront, Mystic Arts World, to remote desert and island supply lines—effectively dismantling an organization that had once seen itself as a "church of psychedelics" tasked with spreading what they called the sacrament of LSD.[69] For the Nixon administration, the Brotherhood's vision of global awakening was reframed as organized crime; their sacrament became contraband, their gospel a federal offense. That day marked the Brotherhood's collapse.[70] Smuggling continued on a smaller scale and LSD continued to be manufactured. The Brotherhood were hunted by the government at least until the last arrest as late as 2009.[71]

But Leary was more than a convenient scapegoat. By then, he was a cultural icon whose résumé included a PhD in psychology from UC Berkeley,[72] groundbreaking research at the Kaiser Family Foundation, and authorship of *The Interpersonal Diagnosis of Personality*,[73] which the *Annual Review of Psychology* once called "the most important book on psychotherapy of the year."[74] His notoriety, however, would spring from something far less conventional: his unapologetic embrace of psychedelics as a pathway to spiritual awakening.

The making of "the most dangerous man in America" was a story that began long before Nixon ever uttered the phrase.

68. Office of the Judiciary, "Hashish Smuggling and Passport Fraud."
69. Office of the Judiciary, "Hashish Smuggling and Passport Fraud."
70. Schmidt, "Joint Force Raids Coast Drug Cult," para. 1.
71. Schou, "'Hippie Mafia,'" para. 4.
72. Leary, "Social Dimensions of Personality," 10.
73. Lattin, *Harvard Psychedelic Club*, 18.
74. Stevens, *Storming Heaven*, 186.

Timothy Leary

* * *

"Whenever it was a good trip, I would think, 'Oh my God! We are all one. Death is not something to fear. Life and death walk hand in hand with each other and it's cool!'"

—Brett Gelman[75]

* * *

If MK-Ultra was the government's secret chapel of mind control, then Harvard—at least for a brief, unruly moment—was the cathedral of mind expansion. And its most unlikely high priest arrived in 1959 wearing a tweed jacket and a freshly minted reputation as one of psychology's sharpest minds: Dr. Timothy Leary.[76]

Before he ever stepped into the Ivy League lecture halls, Leary stumbled upon something far more potent than tenure. Remember our discussion on magic mushrooms? Remember R. Gordon Wasson's journey to Mexico, his fateful meeting with María Sabina, and the *Life* magazine article that told the story from his own, deeply flawed perspective?[77] One afternoon, flipping through that very issue, Leary came across Wasson's now-famous 1957 piece, "Seeking the Magic Mushroom."[78] Part travelogue, part ethnography, part confession—it opened a window into a world where fungi were more than food; they were sacraments. Leary read it, and a seed was planted—one that would eventually lead him far beyond mushrooms, into the still more potent realms of LSD.

That seed sprouted in 1960 when he traveled to Cuernavaca, Mexico. There, under the Mexican sun, he consumed his first batch of psilocybin mushrooms. The effect was nothing short of tectonic. Later, he would describe it as "the deepest religious experience of [his] life"[79] and claim he "learned more in six hours than [in] 16 years" as a psychologist.[80] In that moment,

75. Donick, dir., *Have A Good Trip*.
76. Minutaglio and Davis, *Most Dangerous Man in America*, 3.
77. See chapter 5, above.
78. Wasson, "Seeking the Magic Mushroom," 100.
79. Lattin, *Harvard Psychedelic Club*, 41.
80. Ulrich, *Timothy Leary Project*, 21.

the man who had built a career mapping the human mind discovered there were entire continents missing from his map.

Back at Harvard, he couldn't keep this to himself. Together with a charismatic colleague—Dr. Richard Alpert, who the world would later know as Ram Dass—Leary launched the Harvard Psilocybin Project.[81] The premise was deceptively simple: recruit graduate students from seminaries and universities, administer a dose of psilocybin, and have them record their experiences. No wires, no electrodes, no Skinner boxes. Just a mushroom, a notebook, and the human soul.[82]

But what sounded elegant in theory quickly unraveled in practice. For one, Leary didn't limit the work to the sterile walls of a lab. He ran many of the sessions from his own home, blurring the line between research and salon. Officially, the project was for graduate students only, but undergraduates found their way in. And some graduate students were nudged—if not outright coerced—into participating as part of required coursework.

The sacrament was spilling out of the chalice.

What began as an academic exploration of altered states was turning into a kind of extracurricular initiation. And Harvard, for all its centuries of tradition, was not amused. The administration bristled at the rumors, the breaches of protocol, and the uncomfortable truth that their professors were guiding students into realms the university couldn't chart on any syllabus.

In the end, the verdict came down like a gavel. Leary was dismissed for failing to keep his scheduled appointments; Alpert was fired for giving psilocybin to an undergraduate.[83] Two professors exiled—not for heresy exactly, but for breaking the unspoken rule that the gate between the sacred and the secular must stay locked.

What they didn't yet realize was that their expulsion wasn't an ending. It was an ordination—one that would lead them from the measured doses of the laboratory into the uncharted potency of a different sacrament entirely, a substance whose journey would one day run parallel to the very same networks we have already traced—from the surf breaks of Laguna Beach to the shadowed corridors of Operation BEL.

81. Lattin, *Harvard Psychedelic Club*, 211.

82. Lattin, *Harvard Psychedelic Club*, 42.

83. Weil and Russin, "Crimson Takes Leary," para. 9.

Millbrook

* * *

"I kept thinking to myself, there's gotta be more, there's gotta be more. Then I took acid and I thought—wow, I was right, there's a lot more.

—Bill Kreutzmann[84]

* * *

The Harvard firing should have been the end of Leary's academic career. Instead, it was a promotion—not in title, but in myth. The controversy catapulted him, and psychedelics, into the national spotlight. And just as the establishment was slamming the door, a different kind of patron was opening a much larger one—one that would give Leary the space, the resources, and the freedom to take that new sacrament to its furthest edges.

Before the dust had even settled, Leary had struck up a friendship with Peggy Hitchcock, heiress to the Mellon fortune. Her brothers William and Tommy shared her curiosity about the psychedelic frontier, and soon the family was bankrolling not just Leary's experiments, but the supply lines themselves. Among those in the circle was Owsley Stanley, the underground alchemist behind the Grateful Dead's acid, Ken Kesey's Acid Tests, and much of the West Coast scene and whose handiwork would soon pass through Millbrook's gates, linking it to the same underground currents that would later feed the Brotherhood of Eternal Love. In 1963, William purchased a sprawling sixty-four-room estate in Millbrook, New York, turning it over to Leary as a headquarters for psychedelic exploration. In time, the place would be known simply as Millbrook.[85]

And Millbrook drew seekers like a magnet. One of them was Harvard theologian Paul Lee. Lee's story wound through some of my own stomping grounds—St. Olaf College in Minnesota, then Luther Theological Seminary, where he quickly soured on the rigid orthodoxy and intellectual sterility. Paul Tillich's theology cracked something open for him, and before long he was at Harvard Divinity School, earning his PhD and serving as Tillich's teaching assistant.[86] Lee's name appears on the board of the International

84. Donick, dir., *Have A Good Trip.*
85. Lattin, *Harvard Psychedelic Club*, 211.
86. Lee, "Paul Tillich," para. 10.

Federation for Internal Freedom (IFIF),[87] and he was one of the participants in the famous Good Friday Experiment—an attempt to see if psilocybin could act as an *entheogen* in a religious service. That service took place in Marsh Chapel at Boston University, a stone's throw from Harvard Yard, but the question it posed went far beyond any campus: Could a sacrament come in the form of a mushroom?[88]

At Millbrook, that question was about to find a new answer—one written not in the mycelium of psilocybin, but in the crystalline form of LSD.

Leary, for his part, imagined the psychedelic movement as "a full-blown religious renaissance of the young"[89]—without leaders, without dogma, without institutional gatekeepers. Millbrook became a kind of laboratory for that vision.

Nina Graboi, one of its frequent visitors, described it as "a cross between a country club, a madhouse, a research institute, a monastery, and a Fellini movie set."[90] Guests were met at the door by a sign that read: *Kindly check your esteemed ego here.*[91] Inside, however, the scene was anything but unified. Two distinct camps took shape: the party seekers, often orbiting around Ken Kesey's Merry Pranksters, and the mystics, absorbed in marathon meditation sessions.[92]

Kesey's crew had rolled in expecting a nonstop psychedelic carnival. Instead, they found themselves face-to-face with residents who treated LSD not as party fuel, but as a sacrament—the very new sacrament hinted at when Leary left Harvard under the banner of his so-called ordination. For the mystics, each dose was an altar call in liquid form; for the revelers, it was the ticket to a kaleidoscopic playground. "Party or spirituality?" became the unspoken question hanging over the mansion,[93] a question that would echo far beyond Millbrook into the larger story of LSD's place in the culture.

87. Ulrich, *Timothy Leary Project*, 74.
88. Ulrich, *Timothy Leary Project*, 42.
89. Leary, *High Priest*, 133.
90. Graboi, *One Foot In The Future*, 164.
91. Graboi, *One Foot In The Future*, 164.
92. Lattin, *Harvard Psychedelic Club*, 115.
93. Wolfe, *Electric Kool-Aid Acid Test*, 105.

That split—between those chasing transcendence and those chasing spectacle—was more than a philosophical difference. It mirrored the very fault lines in the counterculture itself, cracks the Nixon administration would later pry open and exploit in its War on Drugs.

Those internal tensions, paired with constant police raids, eventually forced Leary to move on. But by then, Millbrook had already sent ripples far beyond the Hudson Valley. Among its visitors were Nick Sand and John Griggs—the latter on a path that would lead directly to the Brotherhood of Eternal Love.[94]

By January 1967, Leary was on stage at the Human Be-In in San Francisco's Golden Gate Park, coining the mantra "Turn on, tune in, drop out."[95] That same year, he moved to Laguna Beach to live with the Brotherhood—that loose-knit band of surfers, smugglers, mystics, and makers of Orange Sunshine LSD.

And this is where the streams converge. The same LSD that leaked from CIA labs into Kesey's Kool-Aid was now sacrament in the hands of a ragtag church without pews—a countercultural order whose mission was equal parts smuggling and salvation. That same acid flowed into the veins of the Brotherhood of Eternal Love, and from there into the hands of Lonnie Frisbee—where it became the unlikely ignition for a Jesus Revolution, knocking him to the ground in a field, weeping in the presence of God. The same psilocybin that had cracked open Leary's religious sensibilities was reshaping the language of spirituality for a generation. And the same mescaline that lifted Aldous Huxley into beatific vision had long been the teacher of Indigenous healers in the desert, carrying a wisdom older than the churches that dismissed it.

If the religious establishment of the 1960s and 1970s knew anything, it was that God did not belong to the hippies, their music, or their psychedelics. And yet—God kept showing up there anyway. Barefoot in the grass. Dancing to the Byrds. Speaking in the strange, sacramental language of acid, mushrooms, and cactus. From the margins, a revival caught fire, smuggling grace in through the back door of the American church.

94. See chapter 2, above.

95. Starbacker, "Tune In, Turn On, Step Up," title.

And here's the thing: history tells us this was not an anomaly. Across the centuries, across continents, nearly every culture has reached for some kind of plant, fungus, or brew when reaching for the divine. From the barley-and-mint potion of the Eleusinian Mysteries to the cactus buttons of the desert, from the vine and leaf of the Amazon to the bread and wine of the Eucharist, the line between sacrament and psychedelic is thinner than we've been taught. Even in the shadows of medieval cathedrals, some fourth-century frescoes hint at mushrooms painted right into the story of Eden.

The Brotherhood wasn't wrong when they called LSD their sacrament. They were standing in a lineage far older than they knew—a lineage in which the "flesh of the gods" was eaten, drunk, and shared as a means of touching what cannot be touched.

Chapter 7

Flesh of the Gods

"For God knows that when you eat of it your eyes will be opened and you will be like God, knowing . . ."
—Genesis 3:4–5

Throughout human history, nearly every culture has held some sacred meal, drink, or plant that opens the eyes to the divine.[1] In that spirit, there's a painting on the wall of a tiny chapel in Plaincourault, France, dating back to 1291 CE.[2]

Before I describe it, let me take you back to a story you probably know by heart—and if not, you've at least heard it in one form or another. It's the story of the garden of Eden.

Genesis 3 tells of a tree in the middle of the garden. God warns Adam and Eve not to eat from it: "You must not eat fruit from the tree that is in the middle of the garden, and you must not touch it, or you will die."[3]

Then the serpent shows up, smooth-tongued, telling them they won't die at all. "You will not certainly die," the serpent said to the woman. "For God knows that when you eat from it your eyes will be opened, and you will be like God . . ."[4]

1. George et al., "Psychedelic Renaissance."
2. Beckstead et al., "Entheogenic Origins of Mormonism."
3. Genesis 3:3.
4. Genesis 3:4–5.

For centuries we've argued over what kind of tree this was. Apple? Pomegranate? Fig?

Now—shift your focus back to that chapel wall in France. The plaster is aged white, the paint a fading red. Two human figures stand on either side—one clearly male, the other clearly female. But the "tree" between them? Not a tree at all. It's a towering, human-sized mushroom. The medieval title calls it simply: Temptation in the Garden of Eden.

So let's replay it. The temptation is: eat from the tree, your eyes will be opened, and you'll know good from evil. But here, the "tree" is a mushroom. And what do we hear over and over about certain mushrooms and other psychedelics? That they open the eyes or open the mind.

One self-described atheist put it this way: "The way I describe it is being bathed in God's love."[5] God's love!

Is that coincidence? Maybe. But Plaincourault isn't the only place where the sacred and the psychedelic share the same frame.

A few miles away, the Abbey of Saint-Savin-sur-Gartempe holds *The Creation of the Stars*. God places the sun and moon in their stations, and just below—framed perfectly—is a psilocybin mushroom, umbrella-shaped, its cap dipping toward the earth.[6]

At St. Martin de Vicq, in *The Purification of Isaiah's Lips* and *Christ's Entry into Jerusalem*, the crowd isn't waving palms—they're standing beneath psilocybin caps. On the west choir wall, the Last Supper unfolds. Judas leans toward Christ, hand outstretched. On the table: knives—the very same knives painted elsewhere in the scene, cutting mushrooms. Instead of bread, mushrooms are laid out. Eucharist. One continuous symbol.[7]

In the *Great Canterbury Psalter*, *God Creates Plants* shows stylized mushrooms sprouting in Eden's greenery.[8] In *Healing of the Lepers*, mushroom caps rise subtly in the background of restoration.[9]

5. Muraresku, *Immortality Key*, 1.

6. Brown and Brown, *Psychedelic Gospels*, 107.

7. Brown and Brown, *Psychedelic Gospels*, 111, 118.

8. Brown and Brown, *Psychedelic Gospels*, Plate 12.

9. Brown and Brown, *Psychedelic Gospels*, Plate 15.

Once, twice—maybe it's nothing. But again and again, in creation scenes, prophetic visions, acts of healing, and the meal that defines Christian worship? That's not random. That's a pattern. And patterns are signs.

Which leaves us here: Is there anywhere God is not, or anything that is not divine? Anything?? Anything at all??? Maybe those medieval artists were saying what the mystics always have—that God's presence saturates creation. That divine encounter isn't locked in the tabernacle or trapped in the text. It's in the soil and the spores. In the bread and the cup. In the fruiting body that rises after rain.

So maybe the "flesh of the gods"[10] has always been about the same thing: tasting eternity. Dying before you die. Seeing through the veil while you still have breath.

That's the kind of talk that gets you labeled a heretic in some pulpits. But in others—older, stranger pulpits—it was called initiation.[11] The Eleusinian initiate drank the *kykeon* (kue-key-yawn), stepped into the telesterion, and emerged forever changed.[12] The early Christian drank from the cup, broke the bread, and heard the promise, "Whoever eats . . . will live forever."[13] Different stories. Same arc.

I'm not here to collapse those differences. I'm here to notice the rhyme. Because if the sacred has always had a taste, maybe it's not the recipe that matters most. Maybe it's the table. And maybe—just maybe—God's been setting that table in more places than we've dared to imagine.

So we'll go there. To the plain of Eleusis. To the upper room in Jerusalem. To the candlelit hut in Oaxaca. To the peyote road in the high desert, the ayahuasca circle in the jungle, the Siberian snow where Amanita caps once hung to dry in pine boughs. Not to flatten them into one myth, but to read them side by side, the way a theosemiotician reads the signs of the times.

Not to prove. To wonder.

Not to convince. To ask the only question that really matters in this space:

10. Furst, *Flesh of the Gods*, xi.

11. Muraresku, *Immortality Key*, 30.

12. Brown and Brown, *Psychedelic Gospels*, 49.

13. John 6:51.

If the divine is everywhere
—and everything
—why not here?

The West

Though we often forget it—or maybe because forgetting keeps things tidy—Western civilization was not born Christian. The democracy, the art, the philosophy, the science we like to claim as our heritage all came from a world that had never heard the name of Jesus. Before Jerusalem. Before Rome. Before Mecca. There was Greece. And before Athens, there was Eleusis.[14]

In the centuries before the first Gospel was even imagined, Eleusis was the spiritual capital of the Greek-speaking world, drawing generations of seekers to its temple. It was where politics and poetry, philosophy and ritual, found a shared center—not in a creed to be believed, but in an experience to be lived.[15]

That legacy did not survive the clash of empires. By the late fourth century AD, the newly Christianized Roman state outlawed the Mysteries and shuttered their sanctuary.[16] When the Emperor Theodosius's decree came, it didn't just close a temple—it rewrote the spiritual DNA of the West. The question it left in its wake still lingers, "are we Greek, or are we Christian?"[17]

The traditional answer goes something like this: the Greeks built the body of the West, but Christianity saved its soul. Like children of divorced parents, we are taught to honor both—while forgetting that the Greeks already carried their own vision of salvation long before the church claimed the term. For two thousand years, their annual rite promised life beyond death, and by all accounts it delivered that promise in ways the initiated swore were real.[18]

14. Muraresku, *Immortality Key*, 25.
15. Mylonas, "Eleusis and the Eleusinian Mysteries."
16. Gibbon, *History of the Decline and Fall of the Roman Empire.*
17. Muraresku, *Immortality Key*, 25.
18. Ruck et al., *Road to Eleusis*, 19–20.

The ruins still whisper of that confidence. Plato, Pindar, Sophocles—all spoke of Eleusis in language thick with transformation and hope.[19] People didn't leave the Mysteries clutching dogma. They left carrying conviction, something bone-deep, something that could make death itself feel less like a curse and more like a blessing.[20]

Then came the great erasure. Temples fell, churches rose. Pagan altars were smashed. Sacred marble was cut and refashioned into crosses. Christianity took the civic, artistic, and philosophical fruits of Greece and grafted them onto itself, while condemning the old gods and their rites as demonic. Both Greek and Christian identities survived—but their relationship hardened into a fault line. From the Renaissance to the Reformation, from Enlightenment science to modern culture wars, that fault line has been the stage for debates about reason and faith, science and religion, body and soul.

It's along that fault line that we return to Eleusis. Not as antiquarian tourists looking for relics. Not to flatten differences into one story. But as readers of signs, asking whether the "religion with no name"—that underground current of direct encounter with the divine—might still be flowing, unseen, beneath our own age.[21]

If that current exists, Eleusis is one of the last places we can see it clearly before it disappears from view—only to resurface in another upstairs room, in another city, in another kind of feast.

Eleusis

Eleusis sits fourteen miles northwest of Athens, where the land finally exhales into the blue of the Saronic Gulf. The Sacred Way—*Hiera Hodos*[22]—ends here.

It's the same phrase the Gospels will later echo, not in Greek marble, but in Jerusalem's dust: a way made sacred by footsteps, sorrow, and hope. The *Via Dolorosa*—the Way of Suffering—will lead to a different kind of hill, a different kind of altar. Two roads, two cities, two pilgrimages. One ends with the torchlit unveiling of a goddess. The other with a cross.

19. Ruck et al., *Road to Eleusis*, 27–8.
20. Ruck et al., *Road to Eleusis*, 15.
21. Muraresku, *Immortality Key*, 215216.
22. Kerényi, *Eleusis*, 67.

For the ancient Greeks, this was more than a point on a map. It was pilgrimage's last breath before crossing the threshold into the most celebrated and fiercely guarded rites of the ancient world, dedicated to Demeter and Persephone.[23]

For nearly two thousand years—from roughly 1500 BC until the late fourth century AD—people came here not to be instructed, but to be altered. They came to step into something that would mark them for the rest of their lives. You didn't travel to hear good advice.

You came to be changed.[24]

The Mysteries unfolded in two movements. First, the preliminary rites in Athens. Then, the long, deliberate walk—a liturgy in motion—along the *Hiera Hodos*, stopping at shrines, touching mythic markers, reenacting Demeter's search for her stolen daughter, Persephone.[25] Every step was ritual. Every pause was a signpost. The road itself was a sacrament.

At journey's end, the telesterion—a vast, enclosed hall for thousands. Not a temple as we imagine them, all columns and sunlight, but a sealed sanctuary. No pulpit. No pews. A room built for encounter, not explanation.[26]

The rites here were guarded by two figures at the very heart of Eleusinian tradition. The first was the *hierophant*—literally, "he who reveals the sacred things"—the high priest whose task was not to explain the mystery but to unveil it, to stand at the thin place where the seen and unseen meet and usher you across.[27] The second was the *dadouchos*—"the torchbearer"—who carried both literal flame and symbolic light, leading processions and casting illumination on the sacred drama.[28] Both offices were hereditary,

23. Muraresku, *Immortality Key*, 41. The myth is old and spare. Demeter—goddess of grain, mother of harvest—had a daughter, Persephone. The earth cracked open and Hades dragged Persephone into the underworld. Demeter stopped everything: crops failed, winter came and wouldn't leave. Until a bargain was struck—Persephone would return, but only that part of the year. For the rest of the year, she stayed below. Spring, winter, spring again. Life, death, return. The Mysteries didn't explain that story: they enacted it. You didn't hear about descent and return. You went through it.

24. McKenna, *Food of the Gods*, 121.

25. Patera, "Individuals in the Eleusinian Mysteries".

26. Patera, "Individuals in the Eleusinian Mysteries."

27. Kerényi, *Eleusis*, 17.

28. Kerényi, *Eleusis*, 23.

passed down through the oldest priestly families of Athens, as if the blood itself carried the memory of how to open that door between worlds.

At the center of that encounter stood the *kykeon*—the hinge of the whole initiation.[29] You didn't sip it like wine at a wedding. You drank it after days of fasting, at the exact moment the rite demanded—a thick, earthy mixture poured into a sacred vessel and handed to you as the air in the *telesterion* seemed to hold its breath. More than water and barley, less than pure legend—it was the sacred vessel of transformation. Let me say that again: the sacred vessel of transformation.

In the Homeric world, *kykeon* was peasant fare: water, barley, mint—sometimes cheese or honey.[30] But here, it was something else. Something you fasted for. Walked miles for. Drank in that charged moment between the *legomena*—the "things said," the sacred words whispered to prepare you—and the *deiknymena*—the "things shown," the climactic vision at the heart of the rite. Words to open the mind. Vision to seal it.[31] And the *kykeon* was the hinge between them.

For decades, scholars have argued that the Eleusinian *kykeon* was not just symbolic. *The Road to Eleusis* makes the case that barley, stored in the damp Mediterranean climate, often carried *Claviceps purpurea*—ergot.[32] Remember ergot? And not just any ergot, but the same fungal source Albert Hofmann would one day use to synthesize LSD in 1938. Carelessly prepared, ergot could kill or maim. Skillfully prepared, it could yield water-soluble alkaloids—psychoactive cousins of LSD. These compounds could bend perception, dissolve the self, and open sensory floodgates Hofmann himself speculated that other ergot species, like *Claviceps paspali*, might have produced visions rivaling those of Amazonian ayahuasca.[33] And this isn't just theory—archaeologists have found ergot residues in a chalice and in the dental plaque of human remains at a site in Girona, Spain, linked to Eleusinian-style ritual.[34]

29. Kerényi, *Eleusis*, 40–41.
30. Homer, *Iliad of Homer*, XI:624–43.
31. Kerényi, *Eleusis*, 96–97.
32. Ruck et al., *Road to Eleusis*, 15–16.
33. Ruck et al., *Road to Eleusis*, 10.
34. Samorini, "Oldest Archeological Data," 63–80.

Was it psychedelic? The signs sure point in that direction. The recipe is lost, but if Hofmann was right, the *kykeon* could have been, in chemical fact, ancient Greece's own Orange Sunshine.

Fasting came first—an intentional emptying, a clearing of the body's noise—sharpening whatever the *kykeon* carried.[35] It was, in modern terms, preparing the *set*—your inner posture, your readiness to receive. Then, inside the *telesterion*, the rite unfolded through three currents I have already mentioned: the *legomena*—"things said," sacred words spoken to frame and focus the mind; the *dromena*—"things done," the enacted myths and ritual movements that brought the story into your body; and the *deiknymena*—"things shown," the climactic unveiling of the sacred vision itself.[36] Sacred words to orient the mind. Sacred actions to engage the body. Sacred visions to flood the senses. It was the ancient version of what psychedelic researchers now call "set and setting," an intentional architecture for a journey that retold, and reactivated, the cosmic rhythm of Persephone's descent and return. Death and rebirth.

Sound familiar?

Muraresku calls Eleusis one of the purest expressions of the "religion with no name"—a spirituality where the divine isn't mediated by dogma, but met directly through a sacrament that actually does something.[37] Not just a metaphor for transcendence, but the engine that gets you there. At Eleusis, that engine was the *kykeon*. Elsewhere, it might be a Mazatec mushroom, an Amazonian vine, or a peyote button prayed over in a tipi.

Different recipes.

Same table.

And here's the fun part: we don't know where this religion went. The rites were silenced in the late fourth century, casualties of Theodosius's purge of paganism.[38] One year, pilgrims walked the Sacred Way as their ancestors had for millennia. The next, the sanctuary was locked, the hierophant's voice stilled, the *kykeon* undrunk.

35. Harrison, "Prolegomena to the Study of Greek Religion," 162.
36. Kerényi, *Eleusis*, 96.
37. Muraresku, *Immortality Key*, xxvi.
38. Muraresku, *Immortality Key*, 25–32.

Did it vanish? Or did it slip underground—merging, mutating, smuggling its sacramental DNA into other traditions? The timing is suspicious: Eleusis falls just as Christianity consolidates Mediterranean power. Was it a clean break, or a handoff?

If the "religion with no name" is a river running beneath history, maybe it didn't end. Maybe it just found a new cup. Bread and wine instead of barley and mint. A chalice in Jerusalem instead of a *phiale* in Eleusis. If so, the real question isn't *did it survive?*—but *where is it now?*

Ancient voices still echo in the stones. Aristotle said initiates came "not to learn something, but to experience something"—and that choice of words matters.[39] You didn't leave with a syllabus. You left with a new way of seeing. Philosophy could teach you about the soul; Eleusis made you feel like you had one.

Plato—who almost certainly drank the *kykeon*—spoke of beholding a "blessed vision" that convinced him of the soul's immortality.[40] Not a theory. A conviction. In the *Phaedrus*, he describes initiates as beholding beauty itself[41]—language that sounds uncannily like what modern neuroscience records when psilocybin quiets the brain's default mode network and the sense of self dissolves.[42]

Pindar called the initiated "blessed" for knowing "the end of mortal life and the beginning of a new life given of God."[43] Sophocles promised that those who had seen the rites would enjoy a better fate in the afterlife than the uninitiated.[44] These are not casual endorsements. They are the testimony of Greece's brightest minds, speaking with the awe of people who had touched something beyond the veil.

If *The Road to Eleusis* is right—that these blessed visions were catalyzed by an ergot-infused *kykeon*—then we're looking at a spiritual technology honed over centuries: pilgrimage to prepare the mind, fasting to sharpen the body, myth to frame the meaning, and a sacrament to ignite the vision.

39. Ruck et al., *Road to Eleusis*, 7.
40. Kerényi, *Eleusis*, 99.
41. Plato, *Phaedrus*, para. 11.
42. Smigielski et al., "Psilocybin-Assisted Mindfulness Training."
43. Muraresku, *Immortality Key*, 27.
44. Muraresku, *Immortality Key*, 28.

And then—silence. The Sacred Way overgrown. The vows of secrecy replaced by imperial erasure.

Which drops us at another table. Another night. Not the *telesterion*, but an upstairs room in a city about to change the world. No barley and mint this time—just bread and wine. The words are just as strange, just as electric: "This is my body . . . This is my blood."[45]

If Muraresku is right, and if the "religion with no name" slipped its thread into the loom of Christian sacrament, this is where the weave tightens. One cup lifted by a hierophant in a hall outside Athens. Another by a rabbi in occupied Judea. Both inviting friends to drink. Both promising some form of life after death.

Did the current leap from one to the other? Or is it just holy coincidence? We can't prove anything. But we can stand in that upstairs room with Eleusis still humming in our bones—the fasting, the pilgrimage, the vision—and feel the rhyme.

Because whether you call it *kykeon* or chalice, the question under both is the same:

Can you taste everlasting life before you die?

The Upper Room

Step through the doorway and the lamplight warms your face. Shadows climb and curl across stone walls. The meal is already in motion—bread broken, wine poured.

On any other year, this would be a Passover feast of memory. Yes, technically this is still Passover, but tonight it's something stranger. Heavier. Jesus' words bend the table into a different shape—not a commemoration of what God once did, but a living doorway into what God has always done, what God is doing now, and maybe, what God will always do:

This is my body. This is my blood.

45. Mark 14:22–24.

Passover was already sacrament—every loaf and cup bound to that night when the children of Israel stepped into freedom.[46] But in Jesus' hands, the symbols refuse to stay still. They are alive. Dangerous. Personal. He doesn't just retell the story. He drags it into the now—into himself. *Take. Eat. Drink.*

This is not only about remembering. It's about ingesting. It's about tasting. It is about seeing.

From here, the earliest Christian communities will treat this bread and wine as more than metaphor. The *Didache* calls them "spiritual food and drink."[47] Paul warns the Corinthians that to eat and drink without discerning the body is to invite judgment.[48] This is matter as meeting place, material as conduit. Is it the rematerialization of *the religion with no name*?

At Eleusis, the barley and mint carried you through. Here, it's wheat and grape. But the logic holds: the sacrament isn't observed from a distance. It's taken in. Metabolized. Allowed to work from the inside out. María Sabina said her mushrooms "carry you there where God is."[49] The Native American church blesses peyote for the same reason.[50] The forms shift. The function—divine encounter through ingestion—remains.

The Eucharist, then, is not merely a reminder of God's presence. In the theology of the earliest believers, it is participation in God's presence. Irenaeus of Lyons, writing in the second century, called the bread and wine "the earthly and the heavenly together."[51] To eat and drink them was to join two realms. Matter and spirit woven into one. A sacred chemistry.

Luther stood firmly in that stream, refusing to let the meal dissolve into mere metaphor. In *The Babylonian Captivity of the Church*, he seized on the word "*is*" in Christ's words—"This *is* my body . . . This *is* my blood"—as literal, not symbolic.[52] For him, Christ's body and blood are truly present *in, with, and under* the bread and wine, not replacing them but joining

46. Exodus 12.
47. Allen, trans., *Didache*, X:7.
48. 1 Corinthians 11:29
49. Wasson, *Wondrous Mushroom*, 28.
50. Stewart, *Peyote Religion*, 33.
51. Irenaeus, *Against Heresies*, IV.18.5.
52. Luther, *Babylonian Captivity*, 38–58.

them.[53] It is a sacramental union, where the physical elements remain what they are, yet by the promise of Christ, they also deliver what they proclaim: forgiveness, life, and salvation.

And chemistry matters—because the moment you place something into your body in the name of God, you've stepped into a territory older than Christianity itself. You've entered that ancient stream where plant, fungus, or drink becomes the threshold—the hinge between here and the holy. Eleusis. Mazatec Oaxaca. Peyote under the Great Plains sky. The Amazonian ayahuasca circle. And now—a borrowed room in Jerusalem.

We forget the scandal here—and it *was* a scandal. In first-century Judaism, the temple in Jerusalem was the sacred axis—God's presence mediated through priest and sacrifice. But on this night, Jesus steps around the temple entirely. No golden altar. No incense clouding the holy of holies. The meeting place with God is a shared cup on an ordinary table. The sacred has slipped its leash. It's no longer bound to one place, one system, one roof. It's wherever the bread is broken and the cup is passed.

In the centuries ahead, church liturgy will frame the Eucharist in gold and grandeur. But in its first form, it is intimate. Personal. And maybe—if we are willing to follow the Eleusis thread all the way—it was also pharmacologically active. Dangerous. Unproven. Potent.

But, that's where the parallels turn provocative: both Eleusis and the Last Supper hinge on ingestion as the trigger for transformation. Both place in your hands a tangible substance, blessed and offered, that becomes the vehicle for divine encounter. For vision. For salvation. For eternal life.

It's that hinge—ingestion as meeting place—that opens our next question: Could the earliest Christians, like the initiates of Eleusis, have shared a cup that did more than symbolize presence? Could the f*ruit of the vine* have been part of a much older tradition of sacred chemistry? By sacred chemistry, I mean the intentional pairing of substance and setting so the material world becomes a doorway to the divine.

We don't know. But the pattern is ancient. And the table—whether in Athens or Jerusalem—is still set.

53. Tappert et al., *Book of Concord*, 481–86.

What If?

This is the part where the theories start multiplying. Not the safe, seminary-approved ones that keep between the covers of catechisms, but the kind that wander out of archaeology's neat lines into the wild borderlands of ethnobotany and psychedelic history. The ones that lean in and whisper: *What if?*

One of the most provocative belongs to John Marco Allegro, the Dead Sea Scrolls scholar who, in 1970, detonated his career with *The Sacred Mushroom and the Cross*. His thesis: Christianity began as a fertility cult centered on Amanita muscaria—better known as the classic fairy-tale mushroom with its bright red cap and white spots.[54] You've seen it in *Alice in Wonderland*, on Christmas cards, even in *Super Mario Bros.* Beneath that whimsical look, though, lies a potent psychoactive brew that can distort time, alter perception, and induce dreamlike visions. It's not the same as "magic mushrooms" (*Psilocybe*), but it has its own deep history of ritual use among Siberian shamans and in northern European folk traditions. In Siberia, shamans dressed in those same colors gathered the mushroom each winter, dried it on pine branches like ornaments, and delivered it—sometimes through the smoke hole in a roof—in ritual gift-giving.[55] Symbols migrate. Rituals disguise themselves. Which is why Allegro's provocation still lingers: could the "body" and "blood" of the Eucharist be rooted in a mushroom-centered tradition far older than the church?

Decades later, Jerry and Julie Brown's *Psychedelic Gospels* would make a different—but parallel—case, shifting the hunt for mushroom iconography from the Arctic snows to the sanctuaries of Christendom. They spent years photographing medieval and Renaissance church art across Europe and the Middle East: frescoes, stained glass, manuscript illuminations that seem to place psychedelic mushrooms not in the margins, but at the heart of sacred story. We've already mentioned the chapel at Plaincourault, the "tree" in Eden which is clearly a mushroom and possibly an *Amanita muscaria*.[56] In Canterbury Cathedral, Christ's entry into Jerusalem unfolds above a field dotted with stylized psilocybin caps.[57] Just as the red-and-white of Santa

54. Allegro, *Sacred Mushroom and the Cross*, xix–xxx.
55. McKenna, *Food of the Gods*, 108–9.
56. Brown and Brown, *Psychedelic Gospels*, Plate 5.
57. Brown and Brown, *Psychedelic Gospels*, Plate 6.

might conceal a shamanic past, the Browns suggest that biblical scenes may cloak a psychedelic inheritance—one hidden in plain sight, smuggling the old visions forward under the vestments of the new.[58]

For example, following the semiotic textual breadcrumbs: the Greek *pharmakon* in Revelation—most notably in 18:23, where the fall of Babylon is blamed in part on her *pharmakeia*. Our English Bibles almost always render it "sorcery," a translation that folds it neatly into the realm of magic and witchcraft. But *pharmakon* carries a broader range: it can mean "drug," "potion," "poison," or "medicine," depending entirely on context.[59] The semantic hinge is fascinating. Translate it "sorcery," and the warning is about forbidden spiritual power; translate it "drug" or "medicine," and suddenly you're in the contested space where healing, intoxication, and spiritual encounter blur together. That ambiguity leaves room to imagine that what later generations condemned as dangerous magic may once have been understood as sacramental chemistry—an *entheogenic Eucharist* persisting in Christian practice far longer than anyone assumes.[60]

Terence McKenna, in *Food of the Gods*, pushed the timeline back far beyond cathedrals and chalices. For him, psilocybin mushrooms weren't just a curious footnote in religious art—they were the midwives of the human mind. Somewhere on the African savannas, early hominids encountered these fungi in the dung of grazing animals, and the chemistry began its quiet work: sharpening visual acuity for hunting, deepening group bonding through shared visionary states, catalyzing symbolic thinking. From these altered states emerged the raw materials of culture—language, art, myth, and the first whispers of the sacred. Over millennia, the mushroom's neural fingerprint became part of our cognitive DNA, that deep, almost stubborn human instinct to seek hidden knowledge, to pierce the veil, to know for ourselves what is usually left to the priests.[61]

By the time Christianity appeared, the neurochemical grammar for *ingesting the divine* was already ancient history. Bread and wine were just the latest vestments for a primal hunger—the embodied urge to take in a sacrament that bends perception, dissolves the ego, and opens the self to

58. Brown and Brown, *Psychedelic Gospels*, 35–47.
59. BibleHub, "Strong's Greek 5331. φαρμακεία (pharmakeia)," definition 1.
60. Brown and Brown, *Psychedelic Gospels*, 61.
61. McKenna, *Food of the Gods*, 14–19.

mystery. In this light, a sacrament is not just a memorial or symbol; it is a technology—an interface between the human nervous system and the divine, designed to open channels that are otherwise closed. The materials may shift—mushroom, wine, bread, brew—but the operating system underneath remains startlingly consistent: ingest, transform, awaken.

Which is why the absence of a mushroom in the margins of the Last Supper doesn't settle the question. Mainstream historians will tell you there's no direct evidence that the earliest Christian Eucharist contained psychoactive substances. And they're right—there's no first-century recipe hidden in the catacombs reading "add psilocybin." But as the old historian's caution goes, "absence of evidence is not evidence of absence." From a theosemiotic angle, what matters is the recurring sign: the divine offered in a form you take into your body—and in taking it in, you are changed.

The question isn't whether Jesus served mushrooms at the Last Supper. The question is whether the sacrament he gave—whatever its chemistry—belongs to that deeper human lineage of embodied encounter. If it does, then maybe the hard wall we've built between "sacred" sacraments and "profane" psychedelics says more about us than it does about God.

Which is why, before dismissing the possibility, we should notice how naturally the pattern reemerged in the twentieth century—not in a cathedral or monastery, but in the sun-bleached enclaves of Southern California. A place where sacraments traded stone altars for surfboards, and liturgy for the language of the tide. Where the breaking of bread might just happen with bare feet in the sand, and the cup might carry more than wine. Where the old hunger found new skin—and the table of the Lord stretched farther than anyone thought it could.

From Eleusis to Laguna: The Brotherhood of Eternal Love

And now we come full circle back to the Brotherhood of Eternal Love.

If the "religion with no name" had a West Coast chapter, it didn't arrive in marble halls or incense clouds—it came in salt spray and sunburn, rolling in with the tide. Its priests wore board shorts instead of vestments, stood astride surfboards instead of kneeling at altars, and traded barley-water *kykeon* for a crystalline Eucharist punched into tiny squares of blotter paper.

Remember, Laguna Beach in the late 1960s was, to most of America, a postcard—white sand, perfect waves, maybe a movie star hiding behind sunglasses. But for a few hundred young seekers, it became a saltwater telesterion—Jerusalem-by-the-Sea—a place where the veil between ordinary and holy was as thin as a surfboard's fiberglass skin.

Their creed was simple: chase the divine. Their chosen vehicle was LSD. Why? Because when they ingested, they saw. When they ate, they were given a vision—a flash of that peace and love every hippie poster promised, but in a way that felt carved into their very being. They believed they'd opened the telesterion—not for the purified few, but for everyone. No marble steps, no hierophant's blessing—just the table laid out for the whole world, as wide as the horizon.

It was, in its way, the same grammar we've been tracing—ingest to commune, take in to be transformed. But the Brotherhood's syntax was loud, technicolor, and public. Eleusis had its secrecy; the Eucharist had its guarded chalice. The Brotherhood tore down the curtain and threw the doors wide.

The gravitational center was John Griggs—a local tough guy with a taste for risk. In 1965, he was running with a crew in Anaheim better known for petty crime than mystical insight. Then came the hinge moment: a stolen batch of pure Sandoz LSD. He meant to sell it. But curiosity—or providence—won. He and his friends dropped acid together. That first trip felt less like breaking the law than breaking through reality itself. As *Orange Sunshine* records, Griggs "felt he had met God" that day.[62] The coordinates of his life shifted.

Like Eleusis, the revelation was communal. Nobody walked away the same. This wasn't a party drug; it was a sacrament. They named themselves The Brotherhood of Eternal Love and they meant it. They believed they'd found a chemical key to the kingdom of heaven—and they weren't going to keep it locked away.

In Muraresku's terms, Griggs had stumbled onto another iteration of the engine of transformation[63]—ingestion as communion. The same grammar that had carried torchlit pilgrims into the telesterion at Eleusis was

62. Schou, *Orange Sunshine*, 4.

63. Muraresku, *Immortality Key*, 207.

now at work in an Anaheim garage. The *kykeon* was gone. The amphora was now a Mason jar. But the logic was the same: take in the substance, meet the divine.

Their Jerusalem was Laguna Beach, and their temple was Mystic Arts World—a head shop and gallery on Pacific Coast Highway. Out front, it looked like another psychedelic boutique. Inside, it was altar space. Art. Books. Conversations that pinned you in place for hours. Their gospel: LSD could change the world.

The Brotherhood believed that if enough people took LSD with the right intention, humanity would awaken. Unlike Eleusis, this mystery was for everyone.

That democratization was both their power and their danger. The *kykeon* was brewed in secrecy for the purified. The Eucharist was consecrated in community. The Brotherhood mass-produced Orange Sunshine by the millions. By 1969, doses were moving from Laguna to Europe, Asia, South America.

Here's where Muraresku's hypothesis meets the sunburnt street: the Brotherhood weren't just tripping hippies. They saw themselves in a lineage, even if they'd never read the scholarship. Like Eleusis, they had keepers of the recipe—chemists Nick Sand and Tim Scully. Like the medieval church's hidden mushroom iconography on the walls and floors of cathedrals throughout Europe, they wrapped their sacrament in art, music, and surf myth.

And like every disruptive sacrament before them, they drew opposition. Rome shut Eleusis. The empire hunted the early Christians. The Bureau of Narcotics and Dangerous Drugs launched Operation BEL—Brotherhood of Eternal Love—one of the first coordinated global drug busts.[64] Raids. Arrests. Exile.

Before the fall, there was a season when it felt unstoppable. They dropped LSD from planes over festivals, gave it away at be-ins, and—in their most famous move—handed it out freely at the Christmas Happening on Laguna's Main Beach, a chaotic, neon echo of loaves and fishes.[65]

64. Office of the Judiciary, "Hashish Smuggling and Passport Fraud," 21.

65. McPhate, "LSD, Free Love, and Bulldozers," para. 4.

From a theosemiotic read, the Brotherhood is a study in migration of the sign. At Eleusis, the sign was a cup in the hierophant's hand. In medieval Europe, a mushroom disguised as Eden's tree. In Laguna, a sunburst tab of Orange Sunshine. The syntax holds: God can be tasted. God can be taken in.

Their end follows the same arc. Sacred substances get policed. When the sign threatens the order, the order moves. Griggs died in 1969—not from LSD, but from a drug cut with impurities.[66] Without him, the center buckled. Internal fractures widened. External pressure mounted.

Still, the myth lingers. In some tellings, they were criminals hiding behind mysticism. In others, saints of the counterculture. The truth may be both.

From a theological angle, they leave us with a hard question: if a sacrament is judged not by legality but by its capacity to mediate the sacred, what do we make of a generation who met God on a California beach, the taste of salt and lysergic acid on their tongues?

It's tempting to romanticize—to call them the perfect modern parallel to the mysteries of old. But the comparison has edges. Eleusis lasted two millennia. The Brotherhood's golden age didn't even last a decade. Eleusis kept its brew behind closed doors. The Brotherhood's open-handedness may have been their undoing. Their sacrament became commodity, stripped of context.

And yet—in that brief arc—they carried forward something ancient. The hunger that drew pilgrims to the telesterion, disciples to an upper room, seekers to the Mazatec highlands or the peyote road—that hunger was alive in the waves off Laguna.

That hunger has always been about the same thing: tasting eternity. Dying before you die. Seeing through the veil while you still have breath. The ancients called it the "flesh of the gods." Eleusis poured it into a cup. The church broke it in bread. The Brotherhood wrapped it in sunburst paper and let it dissolve on the tongue.

The recipes change. The tables move. But the sign endures—God, taken in.

66. Schou, *Orange Sunshine*, 191.

Chapter 8

The Talking Ass

Creation, Imagination, and Incarnation

"If there is a God, it's going to be a whole lot bigger and a whole lot more incomprehensible than anything that any theologian of any religion has ever proposed."
—Richard Dawkins[1]

Imagination. The church is starved for it.

Not the surface-level kind that churns out new programs, fresh curricula, or trendier music. What the church needs is a deeper imagination—real, profound, unsettling. The kind that catalyzes theology, pressing it until it bends and stretches. The kind that reshapes not only what we do, but who we are.

If you haven't heard of him, Richard Dawkins is an evolutionary biologist connected to Oxford University. He's a vocal atheist, one of the famed "Four Horsemen" of new atheism alongside Sam Harris, Daniel Dennett, and Christopher Hitchens.[2] In a *Time* magazine conversation with former National Institutes of Health director Francis Collins, Dawkins ends with a surprising assertion: he claims to have an open mind—presumably about God. Then he adds the line that frames this chapter: "If there is a God, it's

1. Van Biema, "God vs. Science," para. 40.
2. Timonen, dir., *Four Horsemen*.

going to be a whole lot bigger and a whole lot more incomprehensible than anything that any theologian of any religion has ever proposed."

. . . bigger and more incomprehensible . . .

What he's essentially saying is that he remains an atheist because no definition of God has ever done the concept justice. For more than two thousand years, the church has too often shrunk God—placing the divine in a box.

A small box. A restrictive box. A box that can be controlled, limited, defined.

Imagination

* * *

"We've lost the imagination to let the mystery shine."
—Wilhelm Pauck[3]

* * *

A while back, when I was listening to far more sermon podcasts than I do now, I came across one from Leonard Sweet at Concordia Seminary's preaching conference.[4] To this day, it remains one of my favorites. Sweet began by introducing the audience to Wilhelm Pauck, a noted Reformation scholar. Pauck taught for decades at Union Theological Seminary in New York and later at the University of Chicago, shaping generations of Protestant theologians with his scholarship on Luther and the Reformation.[5] If you were to play the *degrees of separation* game—think six degrees of Kevin Bacon—Sweet was only one step removed from Pauck, since his own doctoral mentor had studied directly under him. I believe that's where this particular story originated.

The story Sweet told came from Pauck's final days in 1981. Reflecting on the decline of denominationalism, Pauck predicted the church's struggles would continue because, as he put it, "we've lost the imagination to let the mystery shine."

3. Sweet, "Can the Church Survive?"
4. Sweet, "Can the Church Survive?"
5. Pauck, "Wilhelm Pauck."

From there, Sweet pivoted to an unexpected metaphor: video game consoles. He traced the evolution of electronics as a relentless competition in speed, memory, and graphic quality. First came Pong, then the Atari 2600, the Sega Genesis, PlayStation, and eventually the Xbox. Each generation promised to be faster, to hold more, to deliver sharper sound and more vivid graphics. Each tried to dominate the market by being *better* than the competition.

And they were gradually *better*.

Until the Nintendo Wii.

You remember, right? You might even still have one tucked away. I do—though every now and then I have to hunt eBay for spare parts from someone off-loading used components. The Wii was, and still is, a great family video game console. Unlike the old controllers tethered to cords, these were wireless, sensing your movements. You could play tennis, baseball, bowling, archery—dozens of games that required you to actually swing your arm, step, move, bowl. It wasn't just pressing buttons; it was embodied, interactive.

And here's the thing: in its first years on the shelves, the Wii outsold them all.[6]

And . . . it wasn't better. Not faster. Not more storage. Not richer sound. Not crisper graphics. In fact, it was worse by almost every technical measure. A step or two behind the rest of the market. Nintendo wasn't leading in specs or horsepower.

Yet when it launched, it flew off shelves. Outselling every competitor.

Why?

Well, certainly not because it was *better*.

But it was *different*.

And at this point in the sermon, Sweet circles back to that quote from Wilhelm Pauck:

"We've lost the imagination to let the mystery shine."

Imagination.

6. Wunderlin, "Nintendo's Strategy," para. 1.

For the video game industry, it was time to think differently.[7] To imagine something new.

For the church, the call is the same. To imagine God beyond what we've settled for—refusing to be boxed in by our charts, programs, or predictions. As in the days of Pauck's death, and as in 1966 when *Time* posted that stark cover—"Is God Dead?"—the church now finds itself in a moment of decline.

The church must think differently. It must have imagination.

And isn't it true? The best time for something new is often right on the heels of an ending.

When old structures collapse. When the world is shaken. That is when God's people are invited—again—to imagine.

And in one of the oldest stories of Scripture, Israel knew this too. In the wilderness, on the brink of change, their imaginations were raw and restless. And into that moment—when they most needed to see differently—God's voice came from the most unlikely of places.

A talking donkey.

Because sometimes the Spirit breaks in not through prophets or priests, but through the ridiculous, the overlooked, the absurd. Precisely there—imagination is born.

And if psychedelics sound like too far a stretch for the divine, remember: the Bible has already gone further. A talking donkey. The absurdity is baked right into the story.

* * *

"What the word God means is the mystery really. It's the mystery that we face as humans, the mystery of existence."

—Ram Dass[8]

* * *

7. Apple advertising slogan, 1997–2002.
8. Peck, dir., *Ram Dass, Going Home.*

The Talking Ass

The story is about a donkey that talks . . . and it's not from the movie *Shrek*.

It's tucked away in the book of Numbers, part of the Torah. The English title "Numbers" isn't what the Hebrews called it. The Hebrew name is *B'midbar*, which means "in the wilderness."[9] That title is more than geography. Yes, the Hebrews are in the desert after Egypt and before the Jordan. But "wilderness" also carries spiritual weight.

It signifies the space presumed empty, the place where God is not.

* * *

> The Israelites traveled to the plains of Moab and
> camped along the Jordan across from Jericho.
> —Numbers 22:1

* * *

Picture the Hebrew camp as concentric circles. At the very center: the holy of holies, the innermost chamber of the tabernacle, where God dwells.[10] Move outward, and each circle is a little less holy, a little farther from the Presence. Cross the final boundary, and you're outside. You're in the wilderness. Which means you're far from the people, far from the tabernacle, and therefore—so the logic goes—far from God.

This is where we meet Balaam—on the fringe.[11] Not inside the camp. Not near the tabernacle. He's in his own land near the Euphrates, a spiritual mercenary-for-hire summoned by Israel's enemies. If holiness is about nearness to the camp and closeness to the center, then Balaam is as far outside as you can get. And still—it is here, in the wilderness, that the story begins to bend. God is about to break in. But not yet.

Balaam climbs to Bamoth Baal, a high ridge where he can look down on Israel's camp from a distance. It's a perfect exclamation mark for the scandal already in motion. He had been hired to curse God's people—but instead is drawn into a conversation with the very God he is meant to

9. Olson, *Numbers*, 1.

10. Olson, *Numbers*, 20.

11. Numbers 22:1–6.

oppose.[12] And then the line: God came to Balaam and asked, "Who are these men with you?"

God is not only outside the camp but standing with Balaam, the outsider, giving him words to say. God's presence is not safely tucked in the middle where the priests say it belongs. God is on the fringe, and Israel doesn't even know it.

* * *

> The elders of Moab and Midian left, taking
> with them the fee for divination.
>
> —Numbers 22:7

* * *

The scandal deepens. According to Torah, God is encountered when people live within the boundaries of the law—when they are righteous. The law is not arbitrary; it's meant to align human life with God's character. Follow the statutes, and you are righteous, close to God. Break them, and you are unrighteous, cut off.[13] Push beyond the boundary, and you're back in the wilderness—back on the distant fringe.

But Balaam? He's a sorcerer, a diviner. His entire vocation is what Torah explicitly forbids: "Do not practice divination . . ."[14] By every definition, Balaam is unrighteous, unholy, disqualified. By every religious measure, he should be silenced. And yet—it is Balaam who hears God's voice. It is Balaam who enters into dialogue with the Holy One.

So we are left with this jarring conclusion: God shows up in the wilderness *and* with an unrighteous man. God is not playing by the rules of proximity or legality. The story insists: God is free.

But the story isn't finished. If it stopped there—with God showing up in the wilderness and speaking to a sorcerer—it would already be scandal enough. Yet there is still one more step, one more boundary to break. Because if God can be found outside the camp, and if God can speak to someone outside the law, then the next question presses in: how far will

12. Numbers 22:7.
13. Balentine, *Leviticus*, 4.
14. Leviticus 19:26.

God go? How outrageous can revelation get? The answer comes suddenly, absurdly, hilariously.

This is the punch line. The most outrageous move of all. God doesn't just speak *to* Balaam; God speaks *through* his donkey. In the middle of a narrow road, the animal sees what Balaam cannot. Blocked by an angel, pressed against the wall, beaten by his master, the donkey finally collapses. And then—absurdity on full display—God opens its mouth. Words tumble out where only braying should be.[15]

We expect God to work through people. Prophets, priests, maybe even the occasional king. If not through people, then at least through creation in its grandeur—the rush of the sea, the fire of the sky, the solemn beauty of mountains. But this? A farm animal with a voice? It is absurd, comic, scandalous. Holy slapstick. A role reversal so ridiculous it borders on comedy. And yet—it is revelation.

God once again upends every expectation, not only of Israel but of us, too. The divine voice chooses absurdity as its stage. The incarnate presence breaks through in the least likely vessel. A donkey talks—and in that braying absurdity, God is heard.

Which forces the question: what do we mean by "incarnate presence"? Is it limited to the near? The central? That which is close? The priests at the center of the camp would have said yes.

But, no.

And that is the larger pattern. Contrary to the expectations of the faithful, it is often the other, the unexpected, the least likely, and the outsider where God's presence breaks through and God's voice is heard in ways that shift the whole religious landscape. Think about it: a diviner hired to curse becomes a prophet of blessing. A donkey opens its mouth and reveals the word of the Lord. Later, a foreign woman challenges Jesus himself, pressing him to widen the borders of mercy. Over and over, the sacred story reminds us that the divine does not always arrive where we have been taught to look.

Yes, God speaks through priests, prophets, and pastors. But the witness of Scripture also pulls us in the opposite direction—toward the scandal, the

15. Numbers 22:21–41.

absurd, the outsider. God does not stay confined to the categories we build. God shows up in the other, the unexpected, the least likely.

That has been the thread running through these stories: revelation that moves from the outside in. God's presence surfacing where it should not be—out in the wilderness, in the life of an unrighteous man, even in the mouth of a donkey. So why should it shock us if that same pattern erupted again in the "wilderness" of the twentieth century—hippies, psychedelics, even a barefoot kid named Lonnie Frisbee dancing on the cliffs of Laguna Beach?

And if this is what the mystery of God looks like, then we are pressed to recover the imagination to see God beyond our boundaries, labels, and comfort zones. That imagination is what lets us recognize the music that rose from that unlikely fusion—psychedelics and Jesus, Orange Sunshine and guitars—the raw soundtrack of a whole new church movement.

The temptation of every generation of the church is to shrink that mystery into a manageable circle—or box it into the rectangle of the holy of holies—in order to define God in terms that keep us comfortable. But Pauck's dying insight is the warning and the invitation: unless we recover the imagination to let the mystery shine, the decline will continue. With imagination, however, we might see God's presence beyond our circles, beyond our expectations, even in the aftermath of collapse.

And that's the heart of incarnation: the mystery of a God who refuses to stay contained, who keeps showing up in the flesh, in the world, in places no one expected.

Incarnation(s)

Incarnation, after all, is the word Christians use for that scandal: God becoming human in the person of Jesus.[16] The logic for the incarnation is the entire purpose of Anselm's work *Why God Became Man*. He asks the question, "for what reason or by what necessity did God become man . . . and restore life to the world?"[17]

The answer hides within the question itself. Why did God become human? Anselm's answer: to restore life. Incarnation occurred in order to restore,

16. Forell, *Protestant Faith*, 161.

17. Anselm, *Why God Became Man*, 64.

in order to bring life, in order to make something new. Not theory. Not abstraction. Life. Newness. Restoration.

Now—yes, the doctrine of the incarnation is the specific idea that Jesus is both God and human.[18] That's the center. That's the scandal. But the pattern won't sit still.

G. W. F. Hegel understood incarnation to be more broad, not necessarily relating to "an individual and even unique event."[19] In other words: *incarnation* names Jesus, but it also names the way God shows up again and again—through history, through people, through moments that crack the world open.

Think about it. Before Jesus walked the earth, God spoke through prophets. After Jesus ascended, God spoke and worked through "unlearned and ignorant men"[20] in order to reveal the gospel. Centuries later, God would still be speaking—sometimes through voices the church tried to ignore, sometimes through movements it dismissed as profane. God has always been. It is our noticing that is uneven—often fixated on the center, blind to the edges. But again and again, the edges are where presence comes into focus.

We call it ordinary, but it is saturated. We call it fringe, but it is alive with God. What seems like surprise is really recognition—the sudden awareness of a presence that was already there.

As one voice put it, "He must speak to [us] with words and symbols [we] can understand."[21] Or as another framed it, "God clothes himself in created reality and appears to speak. The finite is capable of the infinite."[22]

That is incarnation. Not just then. Not just Jesus. But the ongoing mystery of God's presence—always here, always saturating creation—becoming visible in the least likely of places and the least likely of people. Even in the psychedelic subculture of the 1960s.

18. Origen, *On First Principles*, 109.

19. O'Collins, *Incarnation*, 5.

20. Origen, *On First Principles*, 109.

21. Forell, *Protestant Faith*, 161.

22. Fretheim, *Pentateuch*, 146.

CODA

* * *

"Language . . . provides the categories through which people understand themselves, others, and the larger world."

—Crystal Downing[23]

* * *

In 2021, AppleTV+ released a movie entitled *CODA*.[24] The movie is a coming of age story about a teenage girl named Ruby who is finding her identity apart from her family. The story takes place in the fishing town of Gloucester, Massachusetts and, as you would expect, the family is a fishing family. Every day all four of them get up at 3 AM to prepare the family fishing boat, get out onto the water, and catch their fish in time to get it to market in the afternoon. However, Ruby begins to find her identity apart from her family. She begins to find her identity as a singer. She is discovering not only her calling but her literal voice. You might expect that the story revolves around the stereotypical cultural differences between the blue-collar values and lifestyle of a fishing family and that of a young, budding singer entering the world of the performing arts, but that isn't the twist. The twist is that the family is deaf, every one of them (father, mother, brother) except Ruby. The family can't, and never will, hear Ruby sing.

There is a scene where the family goes to a concert in order to see Ruby sing. Of course, they go to see her sing because they cannot hear anything. The scene at the concert is heart-wrenching and profound. It takes no time at all to realize that the deaf family has no idea what is going on. Because they are not able to hear, they might as well be from a different world. They quite literally speak a different language. At one point the director of the movie chose to bring the viewer (us) into the experience of the deaf family by dropping the sound of the movie entirely. Silence. The viewer can see high school students on stage, lips moving and bodies swaying. Silence. The camera pans to the audience and the viewer can see smiles, tears, laughter, and even applause. Silence. There would have been a complete and total disconnect between the deaf family and everyone

23. Downing, *Changing Signs of Truth*, 15.

24. Heder, dir., *CODA*.

else in the room except there was another language being spoken in the room. There were other signs.

In the midst of the culture of a concert, a deaf family must read a different set of signs to interpret and engage with the world they have entered. During my doctoral work, one of my classmates reflected in a forum post on the nature of signs, "As semioticians, we really are striving to become historians and exegetes of history, language, and culture . . . Language does have inherent meaning; we can discover this meaning by paying attention to the particularities of time and place." It's a compelling claim. Still, I am not convinced. I am not sure language and signs have inherent meaning—instead, I find myself drawn to the conviction that the meaning of language and signs are dependent on those interpreting them as well as the system in which they are being read.[25] "Meaning is not inherent in a text itself . . . but emerges only as the interpreter enters into dialogue with [it]."[26] The deaf family in the movie, though they could not hear, had learned a way of seeing—a language that works through sight (facial expressions, body language, etc.)—and used it to interpret the world in which they found themselves. Even in a vocal music concert, they could still participate.

And here's the hinge point for us: if the church is to survive, it must do this as well.

In the case of the church, we too must learn a different and increasingly foreign language in order to interpret the world in which the church finds itself. Theologian Jürgen Moltmann once warned, "The more theology and the church attempt to become relevant to the problems of the present day, the more deeply they are drawn into crisis of their own identity. The more they attempt to assert their identity in traditional dogmas, rights and moral notions, the more irrelevant and unbelievable they become."[27] Similarly, if the deaf family asserted their identity (sign language) on and into the vocal music concert, they too would have become irrelevant. Instead, they endeavored to read the signs of the room in order to participate as best they could. However, the desire for the deaf family didn't stop at merely reading the signs granted by sight. One member of the family went a step further.

25. Silverman, *Subject of Semiotics*, 3.

26. Grenz, *Primer on Postmodernism*, 6.

27. Moltmann, *Crucified God*, 7.

Once the concert was over and the family went home, though they did all they could to read the signs of the audience, it was clear that the deaf family members still missed something at the concert. They could certainly follow the behavior of the crowd—the laughter, the applause, the tears—but beneath all that, something else was happening, something a deaf family could not detect. The father in particular longed for more. He wasn't content to simply mimic the audience's reactions; he wanted to experience the sound itself.

While in the dark of night in the backyard of the house, sitting under the stars, the father asked his daughter to sing her song for him again. She began to sing. He placed his hands on her neck to "feel" her voice. He asked her to sing louder and louder so he could experience the vibrations of her voice through touch.

She sang louder and louder still.

The father continued to move his hands on her neck near her vocal cords, searching for the place of deepest vibration, the pulse of resonance.

And when he found it, he understood.

That image lingers.

I wonder if the church is willing to put its hands on this culture in order to experience it more fully, to engage with it more completely, to be in communion with it more intimately. This is my lesson as well as that of the church. Semiotics is clearly about reading the signs of the times, but what I am learning is that it is a bit more than simply reading signs.

It is about incarnation—about stepping close enough to touch, to feel, to let the vibrations of the world move through us. One can certainly gain some understanding and insight from reading signs, but in the case of the church as well as myself, when I read the signs of the times *and* interact with the world and culture, then I will have the possibility to adjust my thinking, my trajectory, my stance, my perspective, and yes, even my opinion in order to follow Jesus' lead into God's future.[28]

28. Sweet, *I Am a Follower*, 22.

Signs

* * *

> "All of us outgrow some of our beliefs. All of us hatch theories in one moment only to find that we must abandon them in the next."
>
> —Kathryn Schulz[29]

* * *

Which brings us full circle, back to the beginning . . . back to Buffalo Springfield.

Do you feel it?

You should, because something is most definitely happenin' here.

Remember the question? It was less a question than a pulse—an alert that something was already stirring beneath the surface, already breaking open in the cracks of American culture. It was then and it is now as well.

We've traced the signs through the covers of *Time* magazine, each one a cultural icon: "Is God Dead?" . . . "The Hippies: Philosophy of a Subculture" . . . "The Jesus Revolution." Each cover was more than glossy print; it was semiotic, a sign of a world in upheaval, a church in decline, and a Spirit breaking loose in places no one expected.

We've followed the strange liturgy of the Brotherhood of Eternal Love: outlaw saints who believed LSD was not just a drug, but a sacrament, a doorway to God. They weren't theologians. They weren't priests. They were kids—broken, searching, stumbling into mystery. And yet they glimpsed what the church so often forgets: that God is not domesticated, not confined, not controllable. "It's God! It's all God!" John Griggs cried under the desert sky, and though his vision burned out too soon, it still leaves us with a haunting sign.

We've seen how that same counterculture collided with the Jesus People movement, how a barefoot hippie named Lonnie Frisbee—tripping on acid and baptized in the Spirit—ignited a revival. We watched Contemporary Christian Music rise from the ashes of psychedelia, guitars replacing

29. Schulz, *Being Wrong*, 9.

organs, rock replacing robes, as the church learned to sing again. Out of chaos, a new melody was born.

All along, the question has remained: What do these signs mean? Are psychedelics the point? Is LSD the key to God? Again. The answer is absolutely not. The message is simpler. Sharper. More dangerous.

The point is this: the church always misses the point.

Again and again, we look in the wrong places. We guard the center. We defend the institution. We clutch the safe, the sanitized, the respectable. We want God under control, under definition, under the roof of our own certainty. But God is never *just* there.

God is always slipping to the edges. Always sneaking into the wilderness. Always pulsing at the fringe.

That's the scandal of incarnation. Not just that God showed up in Jesus two thousand years ago, but that God keeps slipping in through the cracks—in brothels and back alleys, in communes and canyons, in acid trips and altar calls. Luther's theology of Word and Sacrament reminds us that the infinite does not recoil from the finite but chooses to dwell within it—*finitum capax infiniti* (the finite is capable of the infinite).[30] Which means there is no place, no person, no culture too far from the center, too profane, too strange to be saturated with presence.

And the Scriptures hum the same refrain. Jesus leaves the ninety-nine to go chasing after the one lost sheep. He breaks bread with tax collectors and sinners. He does not flinch from touching lepers. He promises the last will be first and the first will be sent to the back of the line. He speaks with a Samaritan woman—outcast twice over, by ethnicity and by gender—and treats her like a theologian. Page after page, the story arcs toward the margins. The edges become altars. The very places we'd least expect are the places God most insists on showing up.

The tragedy is not that psychedelics are portals to God. The tragedy is that the church winces at the edges, allergic to the wildness, too timid to believe God might actually be there. Once again we hear the warning of Wilhelm Pauck echoing in our ears: the church has lost "the imagination to let the

30. Luther, *Luther's Works, vol. 37*, 232–34.

mystery shine." And because we have, we walk past burning bushes with our heads down, blind to the fire that flickers all around us.

But here's the sign, if we're willing to read it. Buffalo Springfield ringing in our ears again.

"Something is happenin' here"—again.

Do you feel it?

Psychedelics are back in the cultural bloodstream—not just in deserts and communes but labs and clinics, hospitals and research centers. The church can shrug again. Or panic again. Or dismiss again. But the questions won't go away. People are aching for transcendence, for belonging, for a brush with the sacred that feels more real than the plastic gods we've handed them.

The real question isn't whether psychedelics will deliver God. The real question is whether the church will have the courage—or the imagination—to notice God already there.

Because if history has shown us anything, it is this: God is not afraid of the edges. God is not confined to the center. God is already saturating the places we least expect.

Do you feel it?

Something is happening once again.

The question isn't just "will the church feel it?"

The deeper question is this: will the church travel that road again—will the church move from LSD to Galilee? Will we dare to take that journey once more?

What will it be today? Eyes up, church. Go therefore—to the fringe, the edge, the outcast, the voiceless, the oppressed, the forgotten and the forsaken, the freak, the pothead, the tripper, the hippie, the Democrat, the Republican, the libertarian, the scientist and the skeptic, the dreamer and the flat-earther, the rich and the poor, the Muslim, the atheist, the agnostic, the gay, the straight, the queer, the trans, the lesbian, the migrant and the refugee, the documented and the undocumented, the captive and the prisoner—every so-called "other" that we carve into categories.

And do not fear—you are not the first. God is already there. God has always been there. God was never absent.

The boundary between sacred and secular was always our invention—our theology, our dogma, our restless need to define and confine. But incarnation has never honored that line.

So take the trip. Not because we are supposed to "save" those people at the edge, but because what we discover there may be the very thing that saves us. Not by hauling us off to some afterlife heaven in the sky, but by cracking open a little heaven here and now. By going to that place, we participate in heaven's eruption on earth—boundary-shattering, wall-crumbling, table-extending heaven. By stepping into those margins, we begin to unlearn the lie of "us vs. them" and finally see that the divine is everywhere, shimmering in everything and every one.

After all, "God" is only the name we've given to the blanket we throw over the mystery, just enough to give it shape . . . never enough to contain it.

Do you feel it?

Epilogue

Signs

If I'm honest about the signs I see, I have to start here: I've been wrong. And I don't say that lightly—just ask my wife. I don't mean I've failed, exactly. More that the signs, those subtle tremors of the Spirit at the edge of history, are pointing me in a new direction.

I am Gen X to the core—born into skepticism, baptized in irony, raised with suspicion of authority. When I entered ministry, I was arrogant about what it would take to move the church forward: to drag her from the Gutenberg world of text into the Google world of image.[1] And, to be fair, that shift still matters. But it's not enough. That conversation is already twenty years old. Today, the signs demand something else. Something riskier. The church must reckon with what it means to be *post-pandemic, post-America, and post-analog.*

And underneath it all is Pauck's haunting reminder: Imagination is the church's most endangered resource.

Post-Pandemic: Touching What Cannot Be Touched

COVID-19 reshaped the world—and the church with it. John's Gospel gives us a haunting resurrection scene. To Mary, Jesus says, "Do not touch

1. Sweet, *Viral*, 12–16.

me."[2] To Thomas, only verses later, "Touch my wounds."[3] Contradiction? Perhaps. Or perhaps the point is that touch itself was never the endgame. Slavoj Žižek put it this way: The resurrection isn't about touching Jesus but touching others because of Jesus.[4]

The pandemic exposed how fragile touch really is. For months, we were forbidden to embrace. Presence became mediated through screens, through absence. And in that vacuum, our fear of the Other metastasized. Not just fear of viral particles but of ideas, perspectives, whole ways of being.

Jacques Derrida once said that true hospitality means welcoming the unwelcome—the allergens of society.[5] But pandemic-scarred churches seem less hospitable than ever—smaller, more insular, polarized. We forgot that community is only holy when it carries us beyond what feels safe.

And here Pauck's lament cuts deepest. We've lost the imagination to see the mystery shimmering in those who are not us.

Post-America: The Flag and the Cross

The day after *Roe v. Wade* was overturned, I scrolled social media and saw the divide in stark relief. Celebration on one side. Grief on the other. Both sides doing the same thing—projecting their vision of reality onto the other, arguing past one another in a kind of cultural ventriloquism.

Willie James Jennings, author of *After Whiteness,* once wrote of Europe's colonial gaze: Europeans believed they could see the peoples of the world better than those people could see themselves.[6] That gaze hasn't vanished. It has only changed clothes. We still assume the right to define the world for others instead of being in conversation with them. And the church, guilty as any empire, claims to carry a world-transforming message,[7] only too often mistakes imposition for mission.

2. John 20:17.
3. John 20:27.
4. Žižek, *Pandemic!*, 1.
5. Downing, *Changing Signs of Truth*, 183.
6. Jennings, *After Whiteness*, 162.
7. Rollins, *Insurrection*, 15.

This is what I mean by *post-America*. The nation will endure, but the myth of a clean wall between church and state is gone. For some, flag and cross have fused into one icon: a Christian nationalism where Jesus is conscripted into the empire's service. For others, following Jesus will mean dissent—becoming countercultural prophets in the shadow of a civic religion gone awry.

Bonhoeffer resisted a state that swallowed the church. Today, I fear the inverse: a church intent on swallowing the state.[8]

And Pauck's words echo again: without imagination, ideology masquerades as faith.

Mystery gets reduced to control.

Post-Analog: The Multiverse and the Burning Bush

Culture has already slipped beyond us. Marvel films catechize the masses in the liturgy of the superhero multiverse. Science tells its own sacred stories—quantum entanglement, AI consciousness, galaxies uncountable. These are not godless tales. They are gropings in mystery. But the language is almost entirely scientific: the *how*, not the *why*.

And the church? Too often, we retreat. We doused the burning bush long ago.[9] We silenced the chatty rocks and whispering trees. Pauck was right—we lack imagination. Instead of pointing toward the fire shimmering behind the multiverse, we keep lighting matches under dead branches. Meanwhile, Jesus has already wandered out ahead—haunting the metaverse, shimmering in algorithms, humming in cosmic background radiation.

The question isn't whether Jesus is present in the post-analog world. He is. The question is whether the church will risk stepping into that conversation, daring to name the mystery that science can measure but never explain.

8. Bonhoeffer, *Cost of Discipleship*, 30–31.
9. O'Gieblyn, *God, Human, Animal, Machine*, 100.

Follow: Where the Signs Lead

I saw a tweet a while back that said this: "This generation isn't leaving the church because they disapprove of Jesus. They're leaving because they're convinced that the church disapproves of Jesus."

That lands like a confession. Because if Jesus is everywhere—descending even to hell, as the creed insists—then every space, every culture, every conversation is already his.[10] Our task is not to drag Jesus into the world but to notice him already there. To follow.

But here's the scandal: following Jesus changes us more than it changes the culture. Evangelism, in the truest sense, converts the evangelist first. That is the paradox of grace—that in loving the world, we are remade by it.

Which brings us back to Pauck. The church's greatest loss is not relevance, not members, not power. It is imagination. Without imagination, mystery lies hidden. With imagination, even the smallest spark becomes sacrament.

So the invitation is simple—and terrifying: to let the mystery shine again. To follow the signs into the post-worlds we fear. To risk touch, risk conversation, risk wonder. To believe—truly believe—that Jesus so loved the world.

So should we.

And maybe, just maybe, if we listen closely, we'll hear it again:

Buffalo Springfield, humming like a prophecy at the edge of history—

"Something is happenin' here."

10. Sweet, *Nudge*, 28.

Bibliography

Adams, Sandy. "A Generation Led to Jesus: Remembering Pastor Chuck, Part 13." *Calvary Chapel Magazine*, December 20, 2023. https://calvarychapelmagazine.org/articles/generation-led-to-jesus-97-p13.

Akers, Brian P., et al. "A Prehistoric Mural in Spain Depicting Neurotropic Psilocybe Mushrooms?" *Economic Botany* 65, no. 2 (February 17, 2011) 121–28. https://doi.org/10.1007/s12231-011-9152-5.

Alcoholics Anonymous. *"Pass It On": The Story of Bill Wilson and How the A. A. Message Reached the World*. New York: Alcoholics Anonymous World Services, 1984.

Aliwat, A. D. *In Limbo*. New York: Altair, 2021.

Allan, Maurice. "God's Thing in Hippieville." *Christian Life*, January 1968, 21.

Allegro, John Marco. *The Sacred Mushroom and the Cross: A Study of the Nature and Origins of Christianity within the Fertility Cults of the Ancient Near East*. Crestline, CA: Gnostic Media Research, 2009.

Allen, G. C., trans. *The Didache: The Teaching of the Twelve Apostles*. London: The Astolat, 1903. https://dn790000.ca.archive.org/0/items/thedidacheooalleuoft/thedidacheooalleuoft.pdf.

Altizer, Thomas J. J. *Living the Death of God: A Theological Memoir*. Albany: State University of New York Press, 2006.

Anselm. *Why God Became Man: And the Virgin Conception and Original Sin*. Translated by Joseph M. Colleran. Albany, NY: Magi, 1969.

Awards & Shows. "Grammy Awards 1980." https://www.awardsandshows.com/features/grammy-awards-1980-228.html.

Balentine, Samuel E. *Leviticus*. Interpretation. Louisville: Westminster John Knox, 2012.

Barthes, Roland. *Elements of Semiology: Roland Barthes*. Translated by Annette Lavers and Colin Smith. New York: Hill and Wang, 1977.

Bauer, Barbara E. "The Compounds In Psychedelic Cacti." *Psychedelic Science Review*, November 1, 2021. https://psychedelicreview.com/the-compounds-in-psychedelic-cacti/.

Baum, Dan. "Legalize It All." *Harper's Magazine*, April 1, 2024. https://harpers.org/archive/2016/04/legalize-it-all/.

BBC News Magazine. "The People Who Take Drugs To See God." Video, August 21, 2016. https://www.bbc.com/news/av/magazine-37101268.

The Beatles. *All You Need Is Love*. Hollywood: Capitol Records, 1967.

Beckstead, Robert, et al. "The Entheogenic Origins of Mormonism: A Working Hypothesis." *Journal of Psychedelic Studies* 3, no. 2 (June 2019) 212–60. https://doi.org/10.1556/2054.2019.020.

Beeler, Christmas. "A Generation Led to Jesus: Remembering Pastor Chuck, Part 4." *Calvary Chapel Magazine*, October 24, 2023. https://calvarychapelmagazine.org/articles/jesus-mov-96-p4.

Bevan, Ronnie. *Brotherhood Hashish: The Story of Ronnie Bevan*. Houston: Mermaid, 2025.

BibleHub. "Strong's Greek, 5331. φαρμακεία (pharmakeia)." Definition 1: sorcery, witchcraft. https://biblehub.com/greek/5331.htm.

Billboard. "Adult Contemporary Music Chart." *Billboard*, October 31, 1992. https://web.archive.org/web/20190929014613/https://www.billboard.com/charts/adult-contemporary/1992-10-31.

———. "Michael W. Smith: Biography, Music & News." *Billboard*. https://www.billboard.com/artist/michael-w-smith/chart-history/hsi/.

Bitchute. "I Learned It By Watching You." October 23, 2023. https://www.bitchute.com/video/9Yj6rruR3DDa/?fbclid=IwAR2-CIEowIwsDiT_O5kZIvCm659uS2hOLidRfu94BbLC21jDTLmaej3IWgI.

Black, David. *LSD Underground: Operation Julie, the Microdot Gang and the Brotherhood of Eternal Love*. Part of the Psychedelic History series. London: BPC, 2022.

Bleyer, Jennifer. "A Radical New Approach to Beating Addiction." *Psychology Today*, May 2, 2017. https://www.psychologytoday.com/intl/articles/201705/radical-new-approach-beating-addiction.

Bonhoeffer, Dietrich. *The Cost of Discipleship*. New York: Touchstone, 1995.

Bonhoeffer, Dietrich. *Letters and Papers from Prison*. Dietrich Bonhoeffer Works 8. Minneapolis: Fortress, 2010.

Bradford, James. "Brotherhood of Eternal Love Timeline." World Religions and Spirituality Project, January 30, 2024. https://wrldrels.org/2024/01/29/brotherhood-of-eternal-love/.

Brotherhood of Eternal Love. "Brotherhood of Eternal Love, History." https://belhistory.weebly.com/.

Brown, Diana. "The Drug Trip That Led Chelsea Handler to Therapy." iHeart, August 14, 2019. https://www.iheart.com/content/2019-08-14-the-drug-trip-that-led-chelsea-handler-to-therapy/.

Brown, Emma. "'Bear' Stanley, Who Made the LSD on Which Haight-Ashbury Tripped, Dies at 76." *The Washington Post*, March 15, 2011. https://www.washingtonpost.com/local/obituaries/bear-stanley-who-made-the-lsd-on-which-haight-ashbury-tripped-dies-at-76/2011/03/15/ABt95Ib_story.html.

Brown, Jerry B., and Julie M. Brown. *The Psychedelic Gospels: The Secret History of Hallucinogens in Christianity*. Rochester, VT: Park Street, 2016.

Brown, Robert McAfee. "U.S. Protestantism: Time for a Second Reformation." *Newsweek*, January 3, 1966, 33–37.

Buckingham, John. "Debunking the Myths—Did Stocks Really Go Nowhere from 1966–1982?" *Forbes*, February 27, 2023. https://www.forbes.com/sites/johnbuckingham/2023/02/24/debunking-the-mythsdid-stocks-really-go-nowhere-from-19661982/.

Buffalo Springfield. *What's That Sound (for What It's Worth)*. Hollywood, CA: Charles Greene & Brian Stone, 1966.

Burleigh, Nina. "A Psychedelic Trip to Timothy Leary's Catalina Resort in Mexico." *The New York Times*, May 6, 2022. https://www.nytimes.com/2022/05/06/travel/mexico-timothy-leary-psychedelics.html.

Bustraan, Richard A. *The Jesus People Movement: A Story of Spiritual Revolution Among the Hippies*. Eugene, OR: Pickwick, 2014.

CBN.com. "Michael W. Smith's Worship Goes Double Platinum." December 10, 2022. https://cbn.com/article/not-selected/michael-w-smiths-worship-goes-double-platinum.

Charters, Ann. *The Beats: Literary Bohemians in Postwar America*. Detroit: Gale Research, 1983.

Chattaway, Peter T. "Documentary of a Hippie Preacher: A Documentary about Lonnie Frisbee, a Key Figure in the Jesus Movement—Interviews: David di Sabatino." ChristianityTodayMovies.com, April 19, 2005. https://web.archive.org/web/20070511081931/http://www.christianitytoday.com/movies/interviews/daviddisabatino.html.

Cho, Diane J. "All the Celebrities Who've Attended Hillsong Church." People.com, November 5, 2020. https://people.com/celebrity/hillsong-church-celebrities-justin-bieber-carl-lentz/.

CIA. Project MK-ULTRA | CIA FOIA $ (2018). https://www.cia.gov/readingroom/document/06760269.

Clarke, Peter B. *Encyclopedia of New Religious Movements*. London: Routledge, 2006.

Cloud, David. "Calvary Chapel and Maranatha Music." Way of Life Literature, 2013. https://www.wayoflife.org/database/calvary_chapel_and_maranatha.php.

Coelho, Terrye. *Father, I Adore You*. Costa Mesa, CA: Maranatha! Music, 1972.

Coker, Matt. "Ears On Their Heads, But They Don't Hear: Spreading the Real Message of Lonnie Frisbee." *Orange County Weekly*, April 14, 2005. https://web.archive.org/web/20070524214855/http://www.ocweekly.com/film/film/ears-on-their-heads-but-they-dont-hear/14935/.

Cornell Law School Legal Information Institute. "42 U.S. Code § 1996a—Traditional Indian Religious Use of Peyote." https://www.law.cornell.edu/uscode/text/42/1996a.

Costandi, Mo. "Looking Back: A Brief History of Psychedelic Psychiatry." *The British Psychological Society*, September 3, 2014. http://www.bps.org.uk/psychologist/looking-back-brief-history-psychedelic-psychiatry.

Csiszar, John. "What an Average Home Cost in the Year You Were Born." GOBankingRates, April 25, 2025. https://www.gobankingrates.com/investing/real-estate/how-much-new-home-cost-year-were-born/.

Cusick, Richard. "George Carlin: *High Times*." *High Times*, February 1, 1998. https://archive.hightimes.com/article/1998/2/1/george-carlin.

Dahl, Henrik. "Skip's Story: The Beginnings of the Brotherhood of Eternal Love." *The Oak Tree Review*, May 9, 2009. https://oaktreereview.com/skips-story-the-beginnings-of-the-brotherhood-of-eternal-love/.

———. "Tim Scully on the Brotherhood and Making LSD with Bear." *The Oak Tree Review*, May 9, 2009. https://oaktreereview.com/a-correspondence-with-tim-scully/.

Daigle, Lauren. *You Say*. Franklin, TN: Centricity-Warner Bros-12Tone, 2018.

DEA Public Affairs. "LSD: The Drug." DEA, April 27, 1999. https://web.archive.org/web/19990427145322/http://www.usdoj.gov/dea/pubs/lsd/lsd-4.htm.

Deely, John. *Four Ages of Understanding: The First Postmodern Survey of Philosophy from Ancient Times to the Turn of the Twenty-First Century*. Toronto Series in Semiotics and Communication. Toronto: University of Toronto Press, 2011.

Di Sabatino, David. *The Jesus People Movement: An Annotated Bibliography and General Resource*. Lake Forest, CA: Jester, 2004.

Di Sabatino, David, dir. *Frisbee: The Life and Death of a Hippie Preacher*. Warren, NJ: Passion River, 2005.

Dobkin de Rios, Marlene. "Ayahuasca—the Healing Vine." *International Journal of Social Psychiatry* 17, no. 4 (December 1971) 256–69. https://doi.org/10.1177/002076407101700402.

Doggett, Peter. *There's a Riot Going On: Revolutionaries, Rock Stars, and the Rise and Fall of '60s Counter-Culture*. London: Canongate, 2022.

Doherty, Brian. "Dead End Kids on Acid." Reason.com, May 23, 2010. https://reason.com/2010/05/23/dead-end-kids-on-acid/?utm_source=chatgpt.com.

Donick, Cary, dir. *Have a Good Trip: Adventures in Psychedelics*. N.P.: Good Trip, 2020.

Downing, Crystal. *Changing Signs of Truth: A Christian Introduction to the Semiotics of Communication*. Downers Grove, IL: IVP Academic, 2012.

Dylan, Bob. *The Times They Are A-Changin': By Bob Dylan*. New York: Columbia, 1964.

El-Seedi, Hesham R., et al. "Prehistoric Peyote Use: Alkaloid Analysis and Radiocarbon Dating of Archaeological Specimens of Lophophora from Texas." *Journal of Ethnopharmacology* 101, nos. 1–3 (October 2005) 238–42. https://doi.org/10.1016/j.jep.2005.04.022.

Elson, John. "Is God Dead?" *Time*, April 8, 1966. https://content.time.com/time/subscriber/article/0,33009,835309,00.html.

Enroth, Ronald, et al. *The Jesus People: Old-time Religion in the Age of Aquarius*. Grand Rapids: Eerdmans, 1972.

Erickson, Melanie. "Michael W. Smith: A Life of Worship." The Billy Graham Evangelistic Association of Canada, May 15, 2023. https://www.billygraham.ca/stories/michael-w-smith-a-life-of-worship/.

Erwin, Andrew, and Jon Erwin, dirs. *The Jesus Music*. Rocklin, CA: K-Love, 2021.

Erwin, Jon, and Brent McCorkle, dirs. *Jesus Revolution*. Atlanta: Lionsgate, 2023.

Eskridge, Larry. "God's Forever Family: The Jesus People Movement in America, 1966-1977." PhD diss., University of Stirling, 2005.

———. *God's Forever Family: The Jesus People Movement in America*. New York: Oxford University Press, 2018.

The Factory. "Amy Grant." April 16, 2024. https://www.thefactorystl.com/artist/amy-grant/.

Fahey, Todd Brendan. "The Original Captain Trips." *High Times*, November 1, 1991. https://archive.hightimes.com/article/1991/11/01/the-original-captain-trips.

Feilding-Mellon, Cosmo, and Connie Littlefield, dirs. *The Sunshine Makers*. N.P.: Persephone, 2017.

Feinberg, Benjamin. *The Devil's Book of Culture History, Mushrooms, and Caves in Southern Mexico*. Austin: University of Texas Press, 2003.

Ferranti, Seth. "The Trippy Life of the LSD Manufacturer Who 'Helped Create the 60s.'" *Vice*, July 28, 2024. https://www.vice.com/en/article/the-trippy-life-of-the-lsd-manufacturer-who-helped-create-the-60s/.

Fiorenza, Francis Schüssler, and James C. Livingston. *Modern Christian Thought: The Twentieth Century*, vol. 2. Minneapolis: Fortress, 2006.

Ford Library Museum. "United States President's Commission on CIA Activities within the United States." June 6, 1975. https://www.fordlibrarymuseum.gov/sites/default/files/pdf_documents/library/document/0005/1561495.pdf.

Fiske, Edward B. "A 'Religious Woodstock' Draws 75,000." *The New York Times*, June 16, 1972. https://www.nytimes.com/1972/06/16/archives/a-religious-woodstock-draws-75000-a-religious-woodstock-explo-72.html.

Forell, George W. *The Protestant Faith*. Philadelphia: Fortress, 1979.

Frecska, Ede, et al. "The Therapeutic Potentials of Ayahuasca: Possible Effects against Various Diseases of Civilization." *Frontiers in Pharmacology* 7, March 2, 2016. https://doi.org/10.3389/fphar.2016.00035.

Freeman, Paul. "The Dark, One-Dog Night of Chuck Negron." *The Mercury News*, August 15, 2012. https://www.mercurynews.com/2012/08/15/the-dark-one-dog-night-of-chuck-negron/.

Fretheim, Terence E. *The Pentateuch*. Interpreting Bible Texts Series. Nashville: Abingdon, 1996.

Frisbee, Lonnie, and Roger Sachs. *The Great Commission: Part Two of Not by Might Nor by Power*. Santa Maria, CA: Freedom, 2019.

———. *Jesus Revolution: Part One of Not by Might Nor by Power*. Santa Maria, CA: Freedom, 2019.

———. *Set Free: Part Three of Not by Might Nor by Power*. Santa Maria, CA: Freedom, 2019.

From Kirk Franklin's Nu Nation. *God's Property*. Inglewood, CA: GospoCentric, 1997.

Furst, Peter T. *Flesh of the Gods: The Ritual Use of Hallucinogens*. Prospect Heights, IL: Waveland, 1990.

George, Daniel R., et al. "Ancient Roots of Today's Emerging Renaissance in Psychedelic Medicine." *Culture, Medicine, and Psychiatry* 46, no. 4 (September 2, 2021) 890–903. https://doi.org/10.1007/s11013-021-09749-y.

George, Jamilah R., et al. "The Psychedelic Renaissance and the Limitations of a White-Dominant Medical Framework: A Call for Indigenous and Ethnic Minority Inclusion." *Journal of Psychedelic Studies* 4, no. 1 (July 1, 2019) 4–15. https://doi.org/10.1556/2054.2019.015.

Gershon, Livia. "The Story Behind 'This Is Your Brain on Drugs.'" JSTOR Daily, October 19, 2022. https://daily.jstor.org/the-story-behind-this-is-your-brain-on-drugs/.

Gibbon, Edward. *The History of the Decline and Fall of the Roman Empire*. Cambridge: Cambridge University Press, 2013. https://doi.org/10.1017/cbo9781139333542.

Gibson, Mary Jane. "This Bicycle Day, Celebrate Albert Hofmann's Psychedelic Discovery." *Rolling Stone*, October 6, 2023. https://www.rollingstone.com/culture/culture-news/bicycle-day-albert-hofmann-lsd-psychedelic-986279/.

Gladwell, Malcolm. "The Cellular Church." *The New Yorker*, September 5, 2005. https://www.newyorker.com/magazine/2005/09/12/the-cellular-church.

Graboi, Nina. *One Foot In The Future: A Woman's Spiritual Journey*. Santa Cruz, CA: Aerial, 2022.

Grammy Awards. "1966 Grammy Winners." https://www.grammy.com/awards/9th-annual-grammy-awards.

———. "Amy Grant Wins Best Gospel Performance, Female." Grammy Awards, February 26, 1985. https://www.grammy.com/videos/27th-annual-grammy-awards-best-gospel-performance-female.

Grammy Museum. "An Evening with Amy Grant." March 25, 2025. https://grammymuseum.org/event/an-evening-with-amy-grant/.

Grant, Amy. *My Father's Eyes*. Nashville: Myrrh, 1979.

Greenfield, Robert. "Owsley Stanley: The King of LSD." *Rolling Stone*, April 18, 2025. https://www.rollingstone.com/feature/owsley-stanley-the-king-of-lsd-82181/.

Gregoire, Carolyn. "Inside the Movement to Decolonize Psychedelic Pharma." proto.life, October 5, 2023. https://proto.life/2020/10/inside-the-movement-to-decolonize-psychedelic-pharma/.

Grenz, Stanley J. *A Primer on Postmodernism*. Grand Rapids: Eerdmans, 1997.

Grob, Charles S. "Psychiatric Research with Hallucinogens: What Have We Learned?" Schaffer Library of Drug Policy, 1994. https://www.druglibrary.org/schaffer/lsd/grob.htm.

Gross, Terry. "The CIA's Secret Quest for Mind Control: Torture, LSD and a 'Poisoner in Chief.'" *NPR*, September 9, 2019. http://www.npr.org/2019/09/09/758989641/the-cias-secret-quest-for-mind-control-torture-lsd-and-a-poisoner-in-chief./.

Grundy, Gordy. "Hippie Noir, Laguna Beach 1969: Orange Sunshine and the Mystic Arts World." *HuffPost*, December 7, 2017. https://www.huffpost.com/entry/hippie-noir-laguna-beach_b_7598116.

Guerrasio, Jason. "Kristen Bell Says She Did Hallucinogenic Mushrooms to Battle Her Depression." *Business Insider*, May 18, 2021. https://www.businessinsider.com/kristen-bell-tried-mushrooms-depression-hallucinogenic-2021-5.

Guzmán, Gastón. "Hallucinogenic Mushrooms in Mexico: An Overview." *Economic Botany* 62, no. 3 (October 23, 2008) 404–12. https://doi.org/10.1007/s12231-008-9033-8.

Hallman, Carly. "Average Gas Prices in the U.S. Through History [Updated]." TitleMax, August 9, 2022. https://www.titlemax.com/discovery-center/planes-trains-and-automobiles/average-gas-prices-through-history/.

Harrison, Jane Ellen. "Prolegomena to the Study of Greek Religion." Internet Archive, January 1, 1970. https://archive.org/stream/prolegomenatostuooharr.

Hartigan, Francis. *Bill W.: A Biography of Alcoholics Anonymous Cofounder Bill Wilson*. New York: Thomas Dunne, 2001.

Hayden, Eric W. "Charles H. Spurgeon: Did You Know?" *Christian History Magazine*, vol. 29, 1991. https://christianhistoryinstitute.org/magazine/article/spurgeon-did-you-know.

Hay, Mark. "The Colonization of the Ayahuasca Experience." *JSTOR Daily*, November 4, 2020. https://daily.jstor.org/the-colonization-of-the-ayahuasca-experience/.

Heder, Siân, dir. *CODA*. Paris: Pathé, 2021.

Hersh, Seymour M. "Huge C.I.A. Operation Reported in U.S. Against Antiwar Forces, Other Dissidents in Nixon Years." *New York Times*, December 22, 1974. https://www.nytimes.com/1974/12/22/archives/huge-cia-operation-reported-in-u-s-against-antiwar-forces-other.html.

Hirsch, E. D., et al. *The Dictionary of Cultural Literacy*. Boston: Houghton Mifflin, 1993.

Hirschfeld, Tim, et al. "Dose-Response Relationships of LSD-Induced Subjective Experiences in Humans." *Neuropsychopharmacology*, October 2023. https://pmc.ncbi.nlm.nih.gov/articles/PMC10516880/.

Hofman, Albert. *LSD, My Problem Child: Reflections on Sacred Drugs, Mysticism and Science*. 4th ed. Saline, MI: Multidisciplinary Association for Psychedelic Studies, 2017.

Holden, Brad. "Hubbard, Al (1901–1982)." HistoryLink.org, August 26, 2019. https://www.historylink.org/file/20830.

Holmes, Pete. *Comedy Sex God*. New York: HarperWave, 2019.

Homer. *The Iliad of Homer*. Translated by Richmond Lattimore. Chicago: University of Chicago Press, 2011.

Hopkins, Jerry, and Daniel A. Sugerman. *No One Here Gets Out Alive*. New York: Warner, 1980.

Hordern, William, and John Godsey. "Review." *Journal of Bible and Religion* 29, no. 1 (1961) 71–72. http://www.jstor.org/stable/1460191.

Hudson, Bob. *Humble Thyself in the Sight of the Lord*. Costa Mesa, CA: Maranatha! Music, 1978.

Huxley, Aldous. *The Doors of Perception & Heaven and Hell*. New York: Harper Perennial, 1954.

———. *Heaven & Hell*. London: Chatto and Windus, 1956.

Inglis, Ian. *The Words and Music of George Harrison*. Westport, CT: Greenwood, 2009.

Irenaeus. *Against Heresies*. Ashland, OR: Beloved, 2015.

Jay, Mike. "What Happened to Mescaline?" Yale University Press, April 12, 2022. https://yalebooks.yale.edu/2019/08/06/what-happened-to-mescaline/.

Jennings, Willie James. *After Whiteness: An Education in Belonging*. Grand Rapids: Eerdmans, 2020.

Jiménez-Garrido, et al. "Effects of Ayahuasca on Mental Health and Quality of Life in Naïve Users: A Longitudinal and Cross-Sectional Study Combination." *Scientific Reports* 10, no. 1 (March 5, 2020) 4075. https://doi.org/10.1038/s41598-020-61169-x.

Johns Hopkins Medicine. "Johns Hopkins Center for Psychedelic and Consciousness Research." https://www.hopkinsmedicine.org/psychiatry/research/psychedelics-research.

Joseph, Mark. "RIP: Larry Norman, the Most Amazing Artist You've Never Heard Of." *HuffPost*, May 25, 2011. https://www.huffpost.com/entry/rip-larry-norman-the-most_b_88451.

Kalamut, Anthony (Southside AdGuy). "This Is Your Brain . . . This Is Your Brain On Drugs—80s Partnership For A Drug Free America." YouTube video, uploaded March 21, 2010. https://www.youtube.com/watch?v=GOnENVylxPI.

Kerényi, Karl. *Eleusis: Archetypal Image of Mother and Daughter*. Princeton, NJ: Princeton University Press, 1991.

Kirkley, William A., dir. *Orange Sunshine*. Amazon Prime, 2016.

———. *Why Don't You Look Into Jesus*. One Way, 1972.

Lafferty, Karen. *Seek Ye First the Kingdom of God*. Costa Mesa, CA: Maranatha! Music, 1972.

Lattin, Don. *The Harvard Psychedelic Club: How Timothy Leary, Ram Dass, Huston Smith, and Andrew Weil Killed the Fifties and Ushered in a New Age for America*. New York: HarperOne, 2011.

Laurie, Greg. "The Long Strange Trip of Lonnie Frisbee." *Harvest*, October 21, 2022. https://harvest.org/resources/gregs-blog/post/the-long-strange-trip-of-lonnie-frisbee/.

———. "Jesus Revolution: Fact or Fiction?" *Harvest*, March 7, 2023. https://harvest.org/resources/gregs-blog/post/jesus-revolution-fact-or-fiction.

Laurie, Greg, and Ellen Santilli Vaughn. *Jesus Revolution: How God Transformed an Unlikely Generation and How He Can Do it Again Today*. Grand Rapids: Baker, 2023.

Leary, Timothy. *High Priest*. Berkeley: Ronin, 1995.

———. *The Politics of Ecstasy*. Berkeley: Ronin, 1998.

———. "The Social Dimensions of Personality—Group Process and Structure." PhD diss., University of California, 1950. https://archive.org/details/leary/leary.300dpi/.

Lee, Martin A., and Bruce Shlain. *Acid Dreams: The Complete Social History of LSD; the CIA, the Sixties, and Beyond*. New York: Grove, n.d.

Lee, Paul. "Paul Tillich: A Reminiscence and Homage." *Medium*, July 6, 2022. https://medium.com/@drpaullee/paul-tillich-a-reminiscence-and-homage-f50239eceeae.

Life Magazine. "Great Jesus Rally in Dallas." June 30, 1972, cover image, story 40–45.

Lin, Tao. "Psilocybin, the Mushroom, and Terence McKenna." *Vice*, July 29, 2024. https://www.vice.com/en/article/psilocybin-the-mushroom-and-terence-mckenna-439/

Luppi, Katherine. "Woodstock of Laguna Revisited." *Los Angeles Times*, April 15, 2016. https://www.latimes.com/socal/coastline-pilot/news/tn-cpt-et-0415-the-christmas-happening-20160415-story.html.

Luther, Martin. *The Babylonian Captivity of the Church, 1520*. Edited by Paul W. Robinson, translated by Erik H. Herrmann. Minneapolis: Fortress, 2016.

———. *Luther's Works. vol. 37, Word and Sacrament III*. Edited by Robert H. Fischer. Philadelphia: Fortress, 1976.

———. *Luther's Works, vol. 53*. Translated by Hans J. Hillerbrand. Philadelphia: Fortress, 1965.

Macbride, Katie. "'I Am Certain That the LSD Experience Has Helped Me Very Much.'" *Inverse* magazine, September 8, 2023. https://fungaonline.com/i-am-certain-that-the-lsd-experience-has-helped-me-very-much/.

Madden, Emma. "Christian Music Is Experiencing a Pop Breakthrough." *NPR*, June 13, 2025. https://www.npr.org/2025/06/13/nx-s1-5430545/christian-music-forrest-frank-brandon-lake-popularity.

Maguire, Peter, et al. *Thai Stick: Surfers, Scammers, and the Untold Story of the Marijuana Trade*. New York: Columbia University Press, 2015.

McDonough, Jimmy. *Shakey: Neil Young's Biography*. New York: Anchor, 2003.

McKenna, Dennis J., et al. "Monoamine Oxidase Inhibitors in South American Hallucinogenic Plants: Tryptamine and β-Carboline Constituents of Ayahuasca." *Journal of Ethnopharmacology* 10, no. 2 (April 1984) 195–223. https://doi.org/10.1016/0378-8741(84)90003-5.

McKenna, Terence. *Food of the Gods: The Search for the Original Tree of Knowledge—A Radical History of Plants, Drugs, and Human Evolution*. New York: Random House, 1993.

———. "The Stoned Ape Hypothesis." *Voices of Esalen*. Lecture, August 22, 1992. https://www.esalen.org/podcasts/terence-mckenna-the-stoned-ape-hypothesis-8-22-92-100423?utm_source=chatgpt.com.

McLaren, Brian D. *A New Kind of Christianity: Ten Questions That Are Transforming the Faith*. New York: HarperOne, 2011.

McLuhan, Marshall. *Understanding Media: The Extensions of Man*. Cambridge: The MIT Press, 1994.

McMillan, Trisha. "Bicycle Day." *Catalyst Magazine*, May 18, 2016. https://catalystmagazine.net/bicycle-day/.

McPhate, Mike. "LSD, Free Love, and Bulldozers: Laguna Beach's 'Christmas Happening.'" *California Sun*, May 15, 2023. https://www.californiasun.co/lsd-free-love-and-bulldozers-laguna-beachs-christmas-happening/.

Merriam-Webster. "Hippie Definition & Meaning." https://www.merriam-webster.com/dictionary/hippie.

Micó, S. Ibáñez, et al. "Rolandic Epilepsy Clinical Variants and Their Influence on the Prognosis." *Neurología (English Edition)* 27, no. 4 (May 2012) 212–15. https://doi.org/10.1016/j.nrleng.2011.07.002.

Minutaglio, Bill, and Steven L. Davis. *The Most Dangerous Man in America: Timothy Leary, Richard Nixon and the Hunt for the Fugitive King of LSD*. New York: Twelve, 2018.

Mohs, Mayo. "The Alternative Jesus: Psychedelic Christ." *Time*, June 21, 1972. https://time.com/archive/6839039/the-alternative-jesus-psychedelic-christ/.

———. "The New Rebel Cry: Jesus Is Coming." *Time*, June 21, 1971, 59–63.

Moltmann, Jürgen. *The Crucified God: The Cross of Christ as the Foundation and Criticism of Christian Theology*. Minneapolis: Fortress, 1993.

Monson, Jordan K. "Jesus People and the Vibe Shift." *Christianity Today*, July 30, 2025. https://www.christianitytoday.com/2025/07/jesus-people-vibe-shift-zoomer-men-conservative-theology-church/.

Mullen, Shaun. "'Captain Al' Hubbard: An Appreciation." Kiko's House (blog), October 27, 2009. https://kikoshouse.blogspot.com/2009/10/alfred-captain-al-hubbard-appreciation.html

Muraresku, Brian. *The Immortality Key: The Secret History of the Religion with No Name*. New York: St. Martin's Griffin, 2023.

Mylonas, George E. "Eleusis and the Eleusinian Mysteries on JSTOR." Princeton: Princeton University Press, 1961. https://www.jstor.org/stable/j.ctt183q0hq.

Nelson, Kolbe. "Prince Harry Says He's Used Psychedelics to Help Cope with Grief." *CBS News*, January 9, 2023. https://www.cbsnews.com/news/prince-harry-psychedelics-60-minutes-2023-01-09/.

New York Times. "C.I.A. Considered Big LSD Purchase." August 5, 1976, 9. https://www.nytimes.com/1976/08/05/archives/cia-considered-big-lsd-purchase-agency-data-disclose-1953-idea-to.html.

Nichols, David E. "Psychedelics." *Pharmacological Reviews* 68 (April 2016) 264–355. https://doi.org/10.1124/pr.115.011478.

Noll, Mark A. "Where We Are and How We Got Here." *Christianity Today*, April 10, 2020. https://www.christianitytoday.com/2006/09/where-we-are-and-how-we-got-here/.

Norman, Larry. *The Great American Novel*. London: One Way, 1972.

———. *Only Visiting This Planet*. London: Solid Rock Records, 1972.

———. *Street Level*. Albany, NY: One-Way Records, 1972.

———. *No More LSD For Me*. Albany, NY: One Way, 1970.

———. *Reader's Digest*. Albany, NY: One Way, 1972.

Novak, Steven J. "LSD before Leary: Sidney Cohen's Critique of 1950s Psychedelic Drug Research." *Isis* 88 (March 1997) 87–110. https://doi.org/10.1086/383628.

O'Collins, Gerald. *Incarnation*. London: Continuum, 2002.

O'Gieblyn, Meghan. *God, Human, Animal, Machine: Technology, Metaphor, and the Search for Meaning*. New York: Anchor, 2022.

O'Shaughnessy, David M., and Ilana Berlowitz. "Amazonian Medicine and the Psychedelic Revival: Considering the 'Dieta.'" *Frontiers in Pharmacology* 12 (May 28, 2021) 639124. https://doi.org/10.3389/fphar.2021.639124.

Office of the Judiciary. "Hashish Smuggling and Passport Fraud: The Brotherhood of Eternal Love." Hearing, Ninety-Third Congress, First Session. October 3, 1973. https://archive.org/details/hashishsmugglingoounit.

Olson, Dennis T. *Numbers*. Interpretation. Louisville: Westminster John Knox, 2012.

Origen. *On First Principles*. Translated by G. W. Butterworth. Notre Dame, IN: Christian Classics, 2013.

Ortiz, Nicole, and Charles V. Preuss. "Controlled Substance Act of 1970." *National Center for Biotechnology Information*, March 24, 2023. https://pubmed.ncbi.nlm.nih.gov/34662058/.

Oxford English Dictionary. "Hippie." https://www.oed.com/oed2/00106398.

"Panorama: The Mescaline Experiment." *SOTCAA*, February 2005. http://sotcaa.org/hiddenarchive/mayhew01.html.

Pareles, Jon. "Jerry Garcia of Grateful Dead, Icon of 60's Spirit, Dies at 53." *New York Times*, August 10, 1995. https://www.nytimes.com/1995/08/10/obituaries/jerry-garcia-of-grateful-dead-icon-of-60-s-spirit-dies-at-53.html.

Partridge, Christopher H. *High Culture: Drugs, Mysticism, and the Pursuit of Transcendence in the Modern World*. New York: Oxford University Press, 2018.

Patera, Ioanna. "Individuals in the Eleusinian Mysteries: Choices and Actions." *Religious Individualisation* (December 16, 2019) 669–94. https://doi.org/10.1515/9783110580853-034.

Pauck, Marion. "Wilhelm Pauck: Church Historian and Historical Theologian 1901–1981 Précis of a Memoir." *Zeitschrift für Neuere Theologiegeschichte (Journal for the History of Modern Theology* 6 (January 1999) 50–68. https://doi.org/10.1515/znth.1999.6.1.50.

Payne, Leah. *God Gave Rock and Roll to You: A History of Contemporary Christian Music*. New York: Oxford University Press, 2024.

Peck, Derek, dir. *Ram Dass, Going Home*. New York: Further, 2017.

Peirce, Charles S., et al. *Collected Papers of Charles Sanders Peirce: Vols. 5 and 6, Pragmatism and Pragmaticism; and Scientific Metaphysics*. Cambridge: Belknap of Harvard University Press, 1960.

Pfister, Donald H. "R. Gordon Wasson—1898–1986." *Mycologia* 80 (January 1988) 11–13. https://doi.org/10.1080/00275514.1988.12025491.

Philpott, Kent Allan. *Awakenings in America: And the Jesus People Movement*. San Rafael, CA: Earthen Vessel, 2011.

Plato. *Phaedrus*. Translated by Benjamin Jowett. New York: Oxford University Press, 2002. https://www.gutenberg.org/files/1636/1636-h/1636-h.htm.

Plowman, Edward E. "Explo '72: 'Godstock' in Big D." *Christianity Today*, April 8, 2020. https://www.christianitytoday.com/1972/07/explo-72-godstock-in-big-d/.

Pollan, Michael. *How to Change Your Mind: What the New Science of Psychedelics Teaches Us About Consciousness, Dying, Addiction, Depression, and Transcendence*. London: Penguin, 2019.

Pollan, Michael, et al. "The Tragic Story of Maria Sabina's Sacred Mushrooms." *To The Best Of Our Knowledge*, October 21, 2023. https://www.ttbook.org/interview/tragic-story-maria-sabinas-sacred-mushrooms.

Powell, Mark Allan. *Encyclopedia of Contemporary Christian Music*. Peabody, MA: Hendrickson, 2003.

Profit, Al, dir. *American Dope: Acid Dreams*. Los Angeles: Indie Rights, 2018. https://www.amazon.com/Amazon-Video/b?node=2858778011&ref_=nav_em__aiv_0_2_3_2.

Rabey, Steve. "Maranatha! Music Turns Twenty." *CCM*, April 1991, 12.

Ramm, Benjamin. "The LSD Cult That Transformed America." *Awaken*, March 7, 2022. https://awaken.com/2022/03/the-lsd-cult-that-transformed-america/.

Reagan, Nancy. "Just Say No." School Safety 3 (Spring 1986) 4–5. https://www.ojp.gov/ncjrs/virtual-library/abstracts/just-say-no.

Reagan, Ronald. "Address to the Nation on the Campaign Against Drug Abuse." September 14, 1986. https://www.reaganlibrary.gov/archives/speech/address-nation-campaign-against-drug-abuse.

Reuters. "Mike Tyson Says Psychedelics Saved His Life, Now He Hopes They Can Change the World." Inquirer.net, May 29, 2021. https://sports.inquirer.net/424407/mike-tyson-says-psychedelics-saved-his-life-now-he-hopes-they-can-change-the-world#.

RIAA. "Gold & Platinum: Heart In Motion." February 20, 2025. https://www.riaa.com/gold-platinum/?tab_active=default-award&se=heart+in+motion#search_section.

Roberts, Randall. "Jesus, Drugs and Rock 'n' Roll: How An O.C. Hippie Church Birthed Contemporary Christian Music." *Los Angeles Times*, October 5, 2021. https://www.latimes.com/entertainment-arts/music/story/2021-10-05/jesus-music-calvary-church-contemporary-christian-documentary.

Rolling Stone. "Peter Green to Emulate Christ?" July 16, 1970. https://www.rollingstone.com/music/music-news/peter-green-to-emulate-christ-236517/.

The Rolling Stones. *Time Is on My Side*. London: London Records, 1964.

Rollins, Peter. *Insurrection: To Believe is Human, to Doubt, Divine*. New York: Howard, 2014.

Rosenbaum, D., et al. "Psychedelics for Psychological and Existential Distress in Palliative and Cancer Care." *Current Oncology* 26 (August 2019) 225–26. https://pmc.ncbi.nlm.nih.gov/articles/PMC6726261/.

Rothman, Lily. "Is God Dead? *Time*'s Iconic Cover at 50." *Time*, April 7, 2016. https://time.com/isgoddead/.

Ruck, Carl A. P., et al. *The Road to Eleusis: Unveiling the Secret of the Mysteries*. Berkeley: North Atlantic, 2008.

Ruffell, Simon G., et al. "Ayahuasca: A Review of Historical, Pharmacological, and Therapeutic Aspects." *Psychiatry and Clinical Neurosciences Reports* 2 (October 2, 2023) 1–20. https://doi.org/10.1002/pcn5.146.

Rvandervest. "Lindsay Lohan Talks About How Ayahuasca Has Changed Her Life." YouTube video, uploaded April 28, 2014. https://www.youtube.com/watch?v=DbmCegvIzuM.

Salter, G. Connor. "Lonnie Frisbee: The First Jesus Freak and Hippie Preacher." Christianity.com, April 7, 2023. https://www.christianity.com/wiki/people/lonnie-frisbee.html.

Samorini, Giorgio. "The Oldest Archeological Data Evidencing the Relationship of Homo Sapiens with Psychoactive Plants: A Worldwide Overview." *Journal of Psychedelic Studies* 3 (March 29, 2019) 63–80. https://doi.org/10.1556/2054.2019.008.

Santana, Carlos, et al. *The Universal Tone: Bringing My Story to Light*. New York: Back Bay/Little, Brown and Company, 2015.

Sarris, Jerome, et al. "Ayahuasca Use and Reported Effects on Depression and Anxiety Symptoms: An International Cross-Sectional Study of 11,912 Consumers." *Journal of Affective Disorders Reports* 4 (April 2021) 100098. https://doi.org/10.1016/j.jadr.2021.100098.

Schiller, Rebecca. "Lauren Daigle Talks Grammy Wins, Capturing Being 'Carefree & Wild' with 'Look up Child': Watch." *Billboard*, February 11, 2019. https://www.billboard.com/music/awards/lauren-daigle-video-interview-2019-grammys-8497737/.

Schmidt, Dana Adams. "Joint Force Raids Coast Drug Cult." *New York Times*, August 6, 1972. https://www.nytimes.com/1972/08/06/archives/joint-force-raids-coast-drug-cult-57-seized-in-a-group-linked-to.html.

Schmidt, Leigh Eric. "Is God Dead? A TIME Cover Turns 50." April 5, 2016. *ARC* magazine, https://arcmag.org/is-god-dead-a-time-cover-turns-50/.

The School of Wesleyan Studies. "Why Should the Devil Have All the Good Tunes?" September 27, 2023. https://wesleyanstudies.org/blog/why-does-the-devil-have-all-the-good-tunes/.

Schou, Nicholas. *Orange Sunshine: The Brotherhood of Eternal Love and its Quest to Spread Peace, Love, and Acid to the World*. New York: Thomas Dunne/St. Martin's, 2011.

Schou, Nick. "'Hippie Mafia' Hash Smuggler Arrested." *High Times*, November 12, 2009. https://web.archive.org/web/20101123070520/http://hightimes.com/legal/ht_admin/6011.

Schulz, Kathryn. *Being Wrong: Adventures in the Margin of Error*. New York: HarperCollins, 2011.

Schäufele, Wolf-Friedrich. "Martin Luther's Occasional Writings: Table Talk, Letters, and Prefaces." *Oxford Research Encyclopedia of Religion*, March 29, 2017. https://doi.org/10.1093/acrefore/9780199340378.013.294.

Scraps from the Loft. "Bob Dylan: *Playboy* Interview (1978)." January 24, 2021. https://scrapsfromtheloft.com/music/bob-dylan-playboy-interview-1978/.

Select Committee to Study Governmental Operations. *Final Report of the Select Committee to Study Governmental Operations with Respect to Intelligence Activities, United States Senate: Together with Additional, Supplemental, and Separate Views*. Washington: U.S. Government Printing Office, 1976.

Shapiro, Ari. "Nixon's Manhunt for the High Priest of LSD in 'The Most Dangerous Man in America.'" *NPR*, January 5, 2018. https://www.npr.org/2018/01/05/575392333/nixons-manhunt-for-the-high-priest-of-lsd-in-the-most-dangerous-man-in-america.

Sherwin, Maya, et al. "Participant Experiences of Icaros (Amazonian Curative Songs) During a Traditional Medicine Ceremony at the Takiwasi Center, Peru." *Journal of Psychedelic Studies* 9 (May 15, 2025) 149–68. https://doi.org/10.1556/2054.2024.00370.

Silverman, Kaja. *The Subject of Semiotics*. New York: Oxford University Press, 1994.

Singer, Rolf. "Mycological Investigations on TEONANÁCATL, the Mexican Hallucinogenic Mushroom. Part I. The History of TEONANÁCATL, Field Work and Culture Work." *Mycologia* 50 (March 1958) 239–61. https://doi.org/10.1080/00275514.1958.12024725.

Smigielski, Lukasz, et al. "Psilocybin-Assisted Mindfulness Training Modulates Self-Consciousness and Brain Default Mode Network Connectivity with Lasting Effects." *NeuroImage* 196 (August 2019) 207–15. https://doi.org/10.1016/j.neuroimage.2019.04.009.

Smith, Chuck, and Hugh Steven. *The Reproducers: New Life for Thousands*. Glendale, CA: G/L Regal, 1972.

Smith, Gregory A. "Decline of Christianity in the U.S. Has Slowed, May Have Leveled Off." Pew Research Center, February 26, 2025. https://www.pewresearch.org/religion/2025/02/26/decline-of-christianity-in-the-us-has-slowed-may-have-leveled-off/.

Smith, Michael W. *Change Your World*. Nashville: Reunion, 1992.

———. *Go West Young Man*. Nashville: Reunion, 1990.

———. *Michael W. Smith Project*. Nashville: Reunion, 1983.

———. *Worship*. Nashville: Reunion, 2001.

Smith, Warren Cole. "Lonnie Frisbee: The Sad Story of a Hippie Preacher. *Medium*, March 7, 2021. https://wsmith-61546.medium.com/lonnie-frisbee-the-sad-story-of-a-hippy-preacher-f586518c27e6.

Starbacker, Stuart Ray. "Tune In, Turn On, Step Up: Second-Wave Psychedelic Ethics." *San Francisco Chronicle*, November 24, 2020. https://www.sfchronicle.com/opinion/openforum/article/Tune-in-turn-on-step-up-second-wave-15749488.php.

Stephens, Randall J. *The Devil's Music: How Christians Inspired, Condemned, and Embraced Rock "n" Roll*. Cambridge: Harvard University Press, 2018.

Stevens, Jay. *Storming Heaven: LSD and the American Dream*. New York: Grove, 1998.

Stewart, Omer Call. *Peyote Religion: A History*. Norman: University of Oklahoma Press, 1993.

Sting. *Broken Music: A Memoir*. New York: Delta, 2005.

Stone, Roxanne. "Carman, Beloved by '90s Evangelical Kids, Was a Pentecostal Showman at Heart." *RNS*, February 24, 2021. https://religionnews.com/2021/02/23/carman-beloved-by-90s-evangelical-kids-was-a-pentecostal-showman-at-heart/.

Stone, Will. "Microdosing and Tripping on Mushrooms Is on the Rise in U.S." *NPR*, June 28, 2024. https://www.npr.org/sections/shots-health-news/2024/06/27/nx-s1-5021788/magic-mushrooms-psilocybin-microdosing-psychedelics-trends.

Sullivan, Mark. "'More Popular Than Jesus': The Beatles and the Religious Far Right." *Popular Music* 6 (1987) 313–26. http://www.jstor.org/stable/853191.

Sweet, Leonard. "Can the Church Survive the Perfect Storm?" Scholarly Resources from Concordia Seminary, 2007. https://scholar.csl.edu/hom/2007/schedule/1/.

———. *I Am a Follower: The Way, Truth, and Life of Following Jesus*. Nashville: Thomas Nelson, 2012.

———. *Nudge: Awakening Each Other to the God Who's Already There*. Colorado Springs: David C. Cook, 2010.

———. *Viral: How Social Networking is Poised to Ignite Revival*. Colorado Springs: WaterBrook, 2012.

Tappert, Theodore G., et al. *The Book of Concord: The Confessions of the Evangelical Lutheran Church*. Philadelphia: Fortress, 1959.

Tendler, Stewart, and David May. *The Brotherhood of Eternal Love: From Flower Power to Hippie Mafia: The Story of the LSD Counterculture*. London: Cyan, 2007.

Thornbury, Gregory. *Why Should the Devil Have All the Good Music? Larry Norman and the Perils of Christian Rock*. New York: Convergent, 2018.

Tillery, Gary. *Working Class Mystic: A Spiritual Biography of George Harrison*. Wheaton, IL: Quest, 2012.

Time. "The Alternative Jesus: Psychedelic Christ." June 21, 1971. https://time.com/archive/6839039/the-alternative-jesus-psychedelic-christ/.

———. "Youth: The Hippies." July 7, 1967. https://time.com/archive/6834539/youth-the-hippies/.

Timonen, Josh, dir. *The Four Horsemen: Discussions with Richard Dawkins*. Washington, DC: The Richard Dawkins Foundation for Reason and Science, 2008.

Turner, John. "Explo '72." *Anxious Bench*, June 7, 2012. https://www.patheos.com/blogs/anxiousbench/2012/06/explo-72/.

Tylš, Filip, et al. "Psilocybin—Summary of Knowledge and New Perspectives." *European Neuropsychopharmacology* 24 (March 2014) 342–56. https://doi.org/10.1016/j.euroneuro.2013.12.006.

US Census Bureau. "Income in 1966 of Families and Persons in the United States." Census.gov, October 8, 2021. https://www.census.gov/library/publications/1967/demo/p60-053.html.

US Department of Energy. "FACT #741: August 20, 2012 Historical Gasoline Prices, 1929–2011." Energy.gov. https://www.energy.gov/eere/vehicles/fact-741-august-20-2012-historical-gasoline-prices-1929-2011.

———. "The Manhattan Project: The Discovery of Fission, 1938–1939." https://www.osti.gov/opennet/manhattan-project-history/Events/1890s-1939/discovery_fission.htm.

Ulrich, Jennifer. *The Timothy Leary Project.* New York: Abrams, 2018.

Unterberger, Richie. *Turn! Turn! Turn!: The '60s Folk-Rock Revolution.* San Francisco: Richie Unterberger, 2015.

Vamvakopoulou, Ioanna A., et al. "Mescaline: The Forgotten Psychedelic." *Neuropharmacology* 222 (January 2023) 109294. https://doi.org/10.1016/j.neuropharm.2022.109294.

Van Biema, David. "God vs. Science." *Time*, November 5, 2006. https://time.com/archive/6596748/god-vs-science/.

Various Artists. *The Everlastin' Living Jesus Music Concert.* Compilation. Costa Mesa, CA: Maranatha! Music, 1971.

———. *Jesus Sound Explosion.* Orefield, PA: Creative Sound, 1972.

Vineyard Churches. "Vineyard Churches." https://www.vineyard.org/.

Vineyard USA. "A Growing Community of Local Churches Committed to the Message & Practice of the Kingdom of God—Vineyard." https://vineyardusa.org/.

Vitello, Paul. "Chuck Smith, Minister Who Preached to Flower Children, Dies at 86." *New York Times*, October 13, 2013. https://www.nytimes.com/2013/10/14/us/chuck-smith-minister-who-preached-to-flower-children-dies-at-86.html.

Walker, Lucy, dir. *How to Change Your Mind.* Episode 1. New York: Jigsaw, 2022.

Ward, Hiley H. *The Far-Out Saints of the Jesus Communes: A Firsthand Report and Interpretation of the Jesus People Movement.* New York: Association Press, 1972.

Wasson, R. Gordon. "Drugs: The Sacred Mushroom." *New York Times*, September 26, 1970. https://www.nytimes.com/1970/09/26/archives/drugs-the-sacred-mushroom.html.

———. "The Role of 'Flowers' in Nahuatl Culture: A Suggested Interpretation." *Journal of Psychedelic Drugs* 6 (July 1974) 351–60. https://doi.org/10.1080/02791072.1974.10471987.

———. "Seeking the Magic Mushroom." *Life*, May 13, 1957, 100–146.

———. *The Wondrous Mushroom: Mycolatry in Mesoamerica.* New York: McGraw-Hill, 1980.

Watt, Donald. *Aldous Huxley: The Critical Heritage.* The Critical Heritage series. London: Routledge & K. Paul, 1975.

Weil, Andrew. *From Chocolate to Morphine: Everything You Need to Know About Mind-Altering Drugs.* Boston: Houghton Mifflin, 2011.

Weil, Andrew T., and Joseph M. Russin. "The Crimson Takes Leary, Alpert to Task." *Harvard Crimson*, January 24, 1973. https://www.thecrimson.com/article/1973/1/24/the-crimson-takes-leary-alpert-to/.

Weiner, Tim. "Sidney Gottlieb, 80, Dies; Took LSD to C.I.A." *New York Times*, March 10, 1999. https://www.nytimes.com/1999/03/10/us/sidney-gottlieb-80-dies-took-lsd-to-cia.html.

Weller, Sheila. "LSD, Ecstasy, and a Blast of Utopianism: How 1967's 'Summer of Love' All Began." *Vanity Fair*, June 14, 2012. https://www.vanityfair.com/culture/2012/07/lsd-drugs-summer-of-love-sixties.

Wikipedia. "1971 in British Music." October 29, 2024. https://en.wikipedia.org/wiki/1971_in_British_music.

———. "Sound." https://en.wikipedia.org/wiki/Sound.

Williams, Dave. "Lunar Orbiter to the Moon (1966–1967)." *NASA*, November 23, 2018. https://nssdc.gsfc.nasa.gov/planetary/lunar/lunarorb.html.

Winkelman, Michael. "Introduction: Evidence for Entheogen Use in Prehistory and World Religions." *Journal of Psychedelic Studies* 3 (June 2019) 43–62. https://doi.org/10.1556/2054.2019.024.

Wittstein, Ben. "The Costs of Goods the Year You Were Born." *Stacker,* November 17, 2020. https://stacker.com/stories/business-economy/cost-goods-year-you-were-born.

Wolfe, Tom. *The Electric Kool-Aid Acid Test.* New York: Picador, 2009.

WorldRadioHistory.com "Billboard Magazine: 1971." https://www.worldradiohistory.com/Archive-All-Music/Billboard/70s/1971/BB1971.pdf.

Wunderlin, Nick. "Nintendo's Strategy to Fight the Console Wars." *VIA Studio*, April 20, 2020. https://via.studio/journal/nintendo-strategy#.

Žižek, Slavoj. *Pandemic! Covid-19 Shakes the World.* New York: Polity, 2020.

www.ingramcontent.com/pod-product-compliance
Lightning Source LLC
LaVergne TN
LVHW090515110826
845146LV00003B/872

9798385246809